Designers' Workplaces

Designers' Workplaces
Thirty-three offices by Designers for Designers
By Beverly Russell
Editor-in-Chief, Interiors

Whitney Library of Design
an imprint of Watson-Guptill Publications / New York

First published 1983 in New York by Whitney Library of Design,
an imprint of Watson-Guptill Publications,
a division of Billboard Publications, Inc.,
1515 Broadway, New York, N.Y. 10036

Library of Congress Cataloging in Publication Data
Russell, Beverly.
    Designers' workplaces.
    1. Office layout. 2. Office decoration. I. Title.
HF5547.2.R87   1983   747′.8523   83-1356
ISBN 0-8230-7492-7

Distributed in the United Kingdom by Phaidon Press Ltd., Littlegate
House, St. Ebbe's St., Oxford

Manufactured in U.S.A.

First Printing, 1983

1   2   3   4   5   6   7   8   9 / 89   88   87   86   85   84   83

Acknowledgments

This book is a result of remarkable synergy, the creative input of many talented people contributing to a whole production. The totality is certainly beyond what any one person could have ever achieved. All the design projects illustrated in the five chapters were previously published in issues of Interiors magazine between 1979 and 1982. Original copy for the projects was contributed by six skillful writers: Pilar Viladas, Maeve Slavin, Daralice Donkervoet Boles, Olga Gueft, Kathleen Pearson and Melissa Sutphen, as well as the author, who edited all the original manuscripts into the book format.

The quality of visual material is obviously as important as the text. Acknowledgment is given in the Guide to Designers and Resources to all the photographers who were responsible for shooting the pictures in the projects. The integration of words and pictures into a dynamic graphic design is surely the most vital process in the creation of any publication. The brilliant design concept for this book came from the masterly hand and mind of Colin Forbes, New York partner of Pentagram. MaryAnn Levesque, a Pentagram staff designer, steered the project through from the early roughs to finished mechanicals with a deft and professional touch. Linda Reale and Su Bernstein at Interiors were the go-betweens who coordinated all the communications. To all these exceptional people, there is only one small word that hardly seems generous enough but is the most the English vocabulary can produce: thanks.

Contents

Introduction

Developments in the workplace and what they mean to you

Making a space work successfully for business comes naturally to the born restauranteur who, without seeking professional design guidance, understands intuitively that ambiance and comfort are as important to the customer as gastronomic satisfaction. It's easy to use a standard for cuisine and measure a sauce or a dessert for taste, texture and appearance, but it's harder to evaluate an appealing environment. Yet without it, the restaurant can be a flop, even with three-star cooking.

As a matter of fact, in *any* commercial situation, not just the restaurant, how people *feel* about where they are sitting and the surroundings in which they are gathered for a particular activity is central to their enjoyment of the task in hand and thus their performance and level of effectiveness at it. So it's good business to add up the psychological "bottom line" when figuring how much to invest in office space. To rigid linear thinkers, an office is an office is an office—a practical configuration of workstations and filing cabinets, spaces for principals and peons, reception area and restrooms, most probably organized along some hierarchical order dictated by old-fashioned conventions.

White collar hails blue
This imposition of order has not proved very successful in terms of office productivity and prosperity. Recently published studies show that white-collar workers are among the lowest per capita producers in the country. Blue-collar workers win hands down. Why?

These studies point to the fact that blue-collar workers, through their well-organized union spokespeople, have had a *say* in their environment.

They have participated in setting up the production line to make the job easier; they have requested recreational spaces for periods between work. They have demanded amenities, cafeterias, sports facilities, shops, and gotten them when they proved to management that the mentally and physically satisfied employee is happier, stays on the job longer and is thus a valuable asset to the company.

Sounds obvious, doesn't it? But look at offices! The news media regularly report walkouts by workers at automated office workstations who complain of backaches, eyestrain and headaches. The corporation that offers in-house dining is still *not* the norm, despite the fact that productivity studies show that lunch hours spent in house mean more work done. Mention a health club to a personnel chief and it will be mostly dismissed as an unreal expectation.

Incredibly, the value of investing in good design that provides the sedentary office worker with proper seating, filing, work surfaces, privacy, acoustical tolerance, adequate lighting and attractive colors that fuel good psychological vibrations has gone unrecognized by "bottom line" financial managers—even though the payback of such equipment, furnishings and amenities can be demonstrated in terms of real dollars in higher productivity and less absenteeism. Could it be, in fact, that within the cathedrals of commerce lies the last vestige of the puritan work ethic? Do the corporate chiefs believe that to *enjoy* the daily grind from nine-to-five is a sin?

Reviewing all the facts, it seems that something was lost when a segment of our society traded the messy factory floor for the more

antiseptic office cubicle. This book focuses on how this environmental shortfall can be regained. The artist's atelier has long been regarded as an attractive, appealing working environment. This is the place where a creative person has fun. Work is not really work but an exciting effort of individual output. The surroundings reflect the personality of the artist. Work tools are assembled to suit idiosyncratic functions.

The designer, being a similarly creative person, tends to work in the same way. As in the artist's atelier, the emphasis is on free-wheeling activity, tools are on hand to do the job, the surroundings reflect the personality of the firm.

Atelier or office?
There is no ambiguity when you walk through the door; the environment conveys a characteristic message about the people and business that operate here. But since designers are members of the commercial infrastructure, their workplaces are less like an atelier and more like an office. There are conference areas where the design team interacts with clients, workstations, filing cabinets and all the other paraphernalia associated with basic office furnishings. But in the design of this workplace, a premium is put on how it looks and functions.

Because nothing ever happens by accident, wherever the designer gravitates and whatever the physical character and materials of the building, the choice signals a significant bundle of beliefs and psychological traits that are transmitted in turn in the designer's creative output.

Strong social concerns may be defined by arrangements of interior spaces. A democratic attitude may be expressed in an open plan where principals and staff are integrated without walls and doors. Conversely, conservatism is shown in a hierarchy of separate offices.

The 33 examples of designers' workplaces in this book provide independent case histories of functional, psychologically motivating offices.

The five categories

Chapter 1, Adaptation, shows six low-rent spaces—two lofts, a former seminary, a windowless attic penthouse and a suburban house. It is obvious that all have been converted to design headquarters very successfully despite unusual location and architecture. Notwithstanding their large volumes, lofts are not necessarily as uneconomic to heat or cool as they might seem. Indeed, in some cases they are less expensive to operate and maintain than spaces in more conventional buildings because they have thick masonry walls that provide extremely effective insulation, both in winter and in summer. Operable fenestration results in natural air conditioning in summer.

In Chapter 2, Flexibility, we see how two fashion designers, a firm of graphic designers, a firm of architects and an interior designer have organized workplaces for quick changes. The conference room that doubles as a dining area helps in stretching limited space and keeping overhead down. So does the showroom that sells clothes one day and can be transformed into a fashion theater on another. A space that is flexible toward people changes makes sense too. When teams are chosen for architectural projects, easy rearrangement of workstation partitions can save time and money.

In the best-selling book *The Third Wave*, author Alvin Toffler describes a future in which many more people will be working from home. Some of them will be linked up to their office headquarters by sophisticated computers or video-communication systems, such as the picture phone, which will enable them to carry on with a job without actually being at the office all the time. Others will be engaged in highly intensive personal work, such as arts and crafts, which can be done from any location and does not require a formal workplace.

A few years ago many free-lance independent designers would have thought a formal office address essential for business credibility. In today's economy it is perfectly feasible to operate from home with credibility and success.

Chapter 3, Prototype, illustrates six examples of designers' workplaces that are a result of "future think." Invitations were issued to each participant to develop a workplace in response to a social need or trend. These were: outdoors-indoors, the interior VIP office space without windows, the residential or *contradential* office, the executive home office, the VIP office with accessibility and the executive woman's office. Like it or not, current research suggests that a female executive exhibits a more feminine taste than a male executive in matters of office design. Each prototype solves the problem with a high level of ingenuity and originality. It's rare that a designer gets an opportunity to express *all* of his or her ideas without some editing from a client. The designers in this chapter all made the most of this chance.

Then Chapter 4, Image, speaks to the special need of projecting a personal business message. Even the desk tops in these eight spaces belonging to three fashion designers, a graphic designer, a furniture designer and three architects are fine-tuned to relay a consistent story of what the firm does and how it does it. And the message needn't necessarily, of course, be extravagant, a word that people tend to associate with image-making. These eight workplaces demonstrate that image has various guises, from richly cluttered to purposefully spare, Art Deco to International Style.

In Chapter 5, Living Office, we get an insight into how five architects, an interior designer, a graphic designer and a multi-talented designer/filmmaker, have arranged their dualpurpose spaces. Lofts, of course, are ideal for this but by no means essential. Of the eight creative minds in this chapter, only two took this route. The others make the most of a railroad tenement apartment, a brownstone basement, an old farmhouse building and a modern apartment. The variety is indicative of the range of flexibility permissible in today's less rigid approach to business.

Designers are intuitive

Like artists, designers are intuitive people. They often just "feel" that something is right without being able to properly explain why. Because they are holistic rather than linear thinkers, they solve problems in brilliant but unpredictable ways. This is why the world needs them. And why the world profits from their genius. Share these 33 workplaces and you will learn something from them that will help you profit in whatever happens to be your enterprise.

Before You Design: A Checklist

When planning, programming and designing any space, it's easy to overlook the crucial interface of people, process and place. Review this professional checklist. You can use it to help identify your business image, to define your objectives and growth for the future and to make sure you haven't overlooked any important planning considerations. Remember, today the prepared professional is the one most likely to succeed in the marketplace.

Physical image

1. What adjective(s) would describe your ideal workplace?
   - ☐ Friendly
   - ☐ Impressive
   - ☐ Comfortable
   - ☐ Luxurious
   - ☐ Organized
   - ☐ Clubby
   - ☐ Unconventional
   - ☐ Traditional
   - ☐ Residential
   - ☐ Cluttered
   - ☐ Spare
   - ☐ Functional
2. What adjective(s) would most express the image you want *to convey to clients?*
   - ☐ Reliable
   - ☐ Cooperative
   - ☐ Creative
   - ☐ Budget-minded
   - ☐ Flexible
   - ☐ Authoritative
   - ☐ Experienced
   - ☐ Conservative
   - ☐ Trendy
   - ☐ Hard-working
   - ☐ Outstanding
   - ☐ International
3. What design style do you find most compatible?
   - ☐ High-tech industrial
   - ☐ Miesian modern
   - ☐ Post-Modern
   - ☐ Respectful restoration
   - ☐ Eclectic restoration
   - ☐ Ad hoc miscellany
   - ☐ Country club

4. What colors do you prefer?
   - ☐ Classic monotone, black, white, gray
   - ☐ Classic neutrals, beige, brown, tan
   - ☐ Post-Modern pastels, terra-cotta, aqua, mauve
   - ☐ Primary De Stijl
   - ☐ Star Trek dark with glitter
   - ☐ Country Club
5. Will you furnish with:
   - ☐ Manufacturers' products
   - ☐ Furniture of your own design, custom made
   - ☐ Recycled or second-hand furniture
   - ☐ Semi-custom furniture
   - ☐ Special collector's items or antiques
6. Given the option, which light do you prefer for work?
   - ☐ Daylight
   - ☐ Incandescent
   - ☐ Fluorescent
   - ☐ Mixture of all three
   - ☐ Mixture of incandescent/fluorescent
7. How much wall space do you need to show you firm's work?
   - ☐ Lots
   - ☐ Little
   - ☐ None at all

Business amenities

8. Do you need a fully equipped conference/presentation room for client meetings with:
   - ☐ Rear-view projection
   - ☐ Front-view projection
   - ☐ Video-cassette recorder
   - ☐ Video-camera equipment
   - ☐ Video-conferencing screens
   - ☐ Built-in microphone system
   - ☐ Remote-control console

9. How important is a fully equipped resource center, i.e., library for product samples, literature, microfiche, etc.?
   - ☐ Very important
   - ☐ Fairly important
   - ☐ Not very important
10. Will your workplace be equipped for in-house dining for clients and staff?
    - ☐ Yes
    - ☐ No
11. Will your workplace be equipped with auxiliary employee amenities, such as:
    - ☐ Gym
    - ☐ Sauna
    - ☐ Medical facilities
    - ☐ Pool/Ping-pong table
    - ☐ Other
12. Will your workplace be equipped with a sound system for music as your work?
    - ☐ Yes
    - ☐ No

Personnel management

13. Given the option, do you believe in a formal office hierarchy with separate offices for principals, smaller offices for middle managers, open offices for others, or do you prefer an informal arrangement with chiefs and Indians more or less equal?
    - ☐ Formal
    - ☐ Informal
14. Do you want one space to perform more than one function (e.g., conference room into dining room)?
    - ☐ Often
    - ☐ Sometimes
    - ☐ Seldom

15. Will you build in flexibility of walls and workstations?
    - ☐ Yes
    - ☐ Some
    - ☐ No
16. Do you believe in a dress code for business, i.e., ties, no jeans, no sneakers?
    - ☐ Yes
    - ☐ No
    - ☐ Sometimes
17. Do you feel that to hold in-house staff get-togethers is useful?
    - ☐ Helps
    - ☐ Tends to waste time
    - ☐ Makes no difference
18. Do you believe in freedom for employees to play their own radios as they work?
    - ☐ Yes
    - ☐ No

Equipment and technology
19. If you have not yet purchased a computer, do you plan to own one in the foreseeable future for:
    - ☐ Word processing
    - ☐ Data storage and retrieval
    - ☐ Computer design, drafting and manufacturing
    - ☐ Cost estimating
    - ☐ Office management
    - ☐ Project management
    - ☐ Space, energy, furniture control
20. Do you plan to take advantage of all the latest communications technology such as telephone modems, satellite long-distance services, electronic mail, video phone?
    - ☐ Soon
    - ☐ When they have a longer track record
    - ☐ Someday

21. In your objective to reduce energy consumption and overhead running costs as much as possible, will you install:
    - ☐ Computerized energy-monitoring device
    - ☐ Window blinds, shutters or other thermal window devices
    - ☐ Operable glazing
    - ☐ Ceiling fans
    - ☐ Wood-burning fireplace or stove
    - ☐ Solar hot-water heating, space heating or cooling
    - ☐ Skylights to admit natural light
    - ☐ Other
22. Will you pay special attention to acoustic control to keep the perceived noise of people, phones and other office equipment to a minimum?
    - ☐ Special attention
    - ☐ No attention
    - ☐ Little attention

Growth
23. Do you plan to add other disciplines to your firm's capability in the future, such as:
    - ☐ Graphic design
    - ☐ Lighting design
    - ☐ Industrial/product design
    - ☐ Facility management
    - ☐ Energy management
    - ☐ Landscape architecture
    - ☐ Architecture
    - ☐ Engineering
    - ☐ Other
24. How many people is this space needed for?
    - ☐ Now
    - ☐ In 3-5 years
    - ☐ In 10 years

25. What kind of promotional materials do you anticipate developing, distributing and storing to market your firm?
    - ☐ Type biographies with list of achievements
    - ☐ Brochures
    - ☐ Slide presentations
    - ☐ Newsletter
    - ☐ Reprints
    - ☐ Other
26. What areas of design work do you anticipate that your firm will develop during the next 5 years?
    - ☐ Residential
    - ☐ Corporate design
    - ☐ Health care and fitness
    - ☐ Institutional/educational/governmental
    - ☐ Financial/banks
    - ☐ Retail
    - ☐ Recreational
    - ☐ Technological, data centers, computerized facilities
    - ☐ Hospitality
    - ☐ Art and cultural centers
    - ☐ Historical renovation
    - ☐ Others

Adaptation

A delapidated loft, mansion, warehouse or even a disused attic space becomes an exhilarating work space in the hands of a creative designer. Here are six exceptional examples.

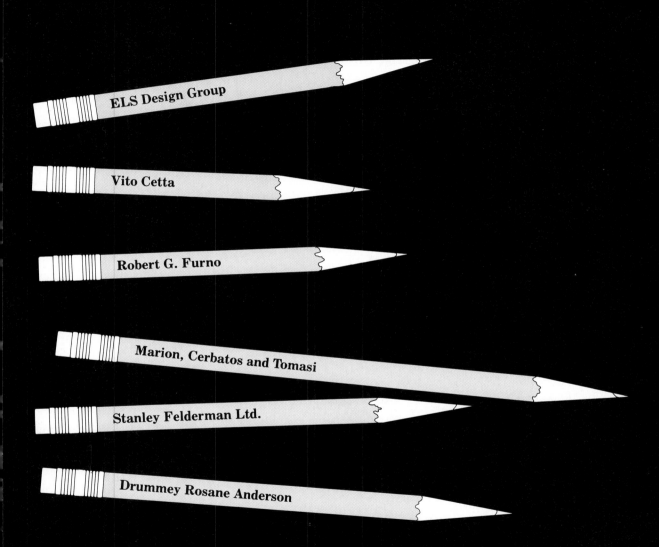

ELS Design Group

Vito Cetta

Robert G. Furno

Marion, Cerbatos and Tomasi

Stanley Felderman Ltd.

Drummey Rosane Anderson

ELS Design Group

A landmark railway building revives from gloomy warehouse to greenhouse atelier.

The old American Railway Express Building in Berkeley, California, had been occupied for many years by a furniture store. To the ELS Design Group, the building's second floor looked like the perfect place for new offices. A large open space was just what the architects wanted, to create an "atelier" atmosphere. They embarked on a drastic remodeling, removing a hung ceiling and cheap paneling, exposing 20-foot ceilings and sand-blasting the brick walls before painting them white. The expansive feeling is preserved by the lack of private offices. Even the conference area has pocket doors that disappear when the room is not in use.

Everything has been done to bring the outdoors in. Motorized skylights in the roof open to admit the mild breezes and introduce enough daylight so that only a minimum of task lighting is needed at workstations. Most impressive is the tree-lined promenade that runs through the length of the space. The combination of openness, natural light, extravagant vegetation and friendly furniture planning has created a working environment so pleasant that employees arrive early and stay late. In office design, that is the highest compliment.

1

2

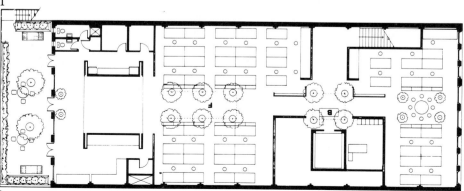

3

Vintage 1920s brick building with 38-foot ceilings provides an opportunity for flights of fancy with a World War II plane hung above the office workstations.

One of the pleasures of adaptive reuse is that it allows for a great deal of imagination. California architect Vito Cetta is one who likes to develop such opportunities fully, and his studio is a remarkable example of recycling. The structure, once a 1920s two-story office building, was found in dilapidated condition. The second story had been knocked out, leaving a space with 38-foot ceilings.

Faced with the luxury of a wide-open space, Cetta decided to fill it with a World War II reconnaissance plane acquired for $1000 and refurbished for an additional $2000. Now hanging from the open rafters, it has the firm's logo painted right on the nose, reminding everyone that this design firm is nothing if not different! Continuing with his recycling project, Cetta obtained doors and windows from a 1920s Los Angeles mansion. Their woodwork restored, they were now integrated in sheetrock partitions that delineate reception area, conference room, library and various workspaces. The furniture was custom made using wood from recycled bowling-alley lanes.

As is so often the case in old existing brick structures, energy consumption in this office is extremely economical. Because of the two-foot-thick walls and California's mild climate, no heating or cooling systems are required: space heaters provide auxiliary warmth when necessary, and operable windows and skylights provide ventilation.

1

2

1.   Architectural elements are painted white
to contrast with the brick of the old structure.
A profusion of plants enhances the organic
spirit of the studio.
2.   Doors and woodwork taken from a 1920s
Los Angeles mansion and inserted into
sheetrock partitions help to create architecture within architecture.
3.   World War II L-4 reconnaissance plane is
suspended above the workspace, a flight of
design fancy made feasible by the 38-foot
ceiling height, in the original found structure.

1. Clerestory windows carefully concealed in the roof of the addition illuminate an expansive drafting room.
2. Except for a large street sign, 17 North Avenue looks like any other suburban house in the neighborhood. Addition is not visible from the front façade.
3. Large curved stair with oak hand-rail recalls the grand stair of the house, which was removed in the expansion process.
4. Floor plan shows office addition, beginning with curved stairway.

Fifty-year-old suburban house gets a face lift and a new life as a design corporate headquarters.

When Albertson Sharp Ewing, Inc., a firm specializing in civil and structural engineering, went looking for new executive headquarters, it found a two-story, 50-year-old house on a site that allowed for attractive remodeling and expansion. Converting such a suburban structure into offices had two advantages: it would preserve the scale of the surrounding neighborhood in Norwalk, Connecticut, and it would provide a comfortable workplace at a cost far lower than that of new construction.

Robert G. Furno, head of ASE/Furno, Inc., the architectural affiliate, was faced with the challenge of designing an 8000-square-foot addition that conformed to a complicated set of zoning restrictions. The addition is exactly the same width as the existing building, and therefore very little of it is visible from the street.

The first floor of the addition houses rentable office space, while the second floors of both new and existing structures house offices for the architectural engineering firm. The former bedrooms of the house are now offices for the firm's partners, the master bath is now the executive bath, and the cedar closet became the photocopying room. In the new wing, the west side contains private offices, while the east side is given over to drafting areas.

Because energy efficiency is an important consideration, both old and new wings are thoroughly insulated and no less than 10 heat pumps allow individual climate controls for various areas. Operable thermal glass with interior blinds achieve efficient window management.

1

2

3

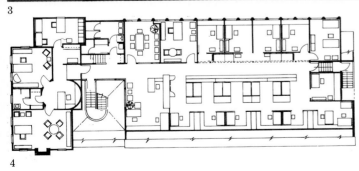

4

Marion, Cerbatos & Tomasi

San Francisco's Western Exchange Building leads a new life with columns and capitals repaired and integrated into a contemporary two-story engineering office.

It is thought-provoking to observe a delightful paradox emerging in design today. The most forward-looking companies now turn to the past for their future. Such is the case for the mechanical and electrical engineering firm of Marion, Cerbatos and Tomasi. Its decision to renovate the Western Exchange Building reflects an appreciation of good design in a structure that has no particular historical significance. The structural integrity of the original telephone company building remained intact, resulting in considerable savings over the cost of a completely new headquarters.

The company chose to occupy only the ground floor and basement of the building and lease out the upper stories. Interconnections between the two work levels were therefore necessary not only for practical but also for spatial reasons.

Designers Marquis Associates cut through the existing floor slabs between the beams to open up the low-ceilinged basement with a light and airy center. The placement of lounge and lunchroom facilities in the basement level emphasizes the inverted relationship of floors; thus the first floor is given the quality of a mezzanine, integrally related to the floor below.

The quality of the original space is carefully preserved in the open arrangement of drafting rooms around the central well. Rather than obscure the decorative column capitals with a hung ceiling, the designers chose to suspend acoustical panels between them. The columnar grid marked by blue plaster contrasts the white panels, while special square lighting fixtures hung from the acoustical "clouds" exaggerate the grid. The fixtures, designed by the in-house team of Marion, Cerbatos and Tomasi, combine up-and-down lighting and complement the natural daylighting afforded by the large perimeter windows.

Clearly the new office arrangement reinforces the character and quality of the original structure. It's a sensitive solution to the particular problems of rehabilitation.

3. Mezzanine level looking toward the resource library.
4. Basement floor plan is organized around the central atrium. Small windows punctuate the shell and bring in additional light.
5. View from the basement looking up to the mezzanine level through the central atrium.

3

4

5

Disused attic turns into an attractive, light-filled, functional space with an intentional sense of playfulness.

Like everyone else in Manhattan, when Stanley Felderman and Alan Felsenthal, principals of Stanley Felderman Ltd., found themselves on the market for a larger office space, they were appalled by the high rents. So it was fortunate that Joseph Fischer of Columbia Pictures Industries, a long-time client, suggested that they investigate the "penthouse" floor of the Columbia building on Fifth Avenue. Far from glamorous, this space turned out to be without windows or elevator, and its walls and ceilings were spotted with partially exposed steel beams, drainage ducts and water pipes.

Nevertheless, the two designers thought the 6500 square feet had potential, so they set about converting it into a good working environment. By demolishing the southern and western walls, they exposed sloping ceilings and created more space and a dramatic visual effect. Exposed steel beams and ductwork were encased and used to define areas of the office. Felderman found, even where the beams and ducts were pleasing to the eye, they improved through encasing and created a playfulness as to which are real structural supports and which are intentional architectural foils.

Faced with the reality of an expanding firm, Felderman wished to maintain the intimacy and interaction of a typical design studio. So he designed a large central area with a few private offices along the perimeter. Sliding glass doors and glass walls insure that the unity between spaces is maintained.

1

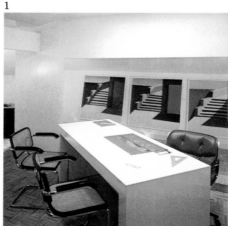

2

3

1. Custom-designed workstations for the drafting room, with flat surfaces adjacent to conferencing.
2. Principal Alan Felsenthal's office, with triptych by Betty Ann Felderman.
3. View from Felderman's executive chair. Wood parquet floor contrasts with leather and cane textures on the seating, which, with plants, emphasize a preference for natural materials.

4. Skylight over the design and drafting areas emits a soft illumination that filters throughout the office.
5. Glass-walled conference room with Pop Art sofa, reception area, beyond.
6. Betty Ann Felderman triptych in Stanley Federman's skylighted office.
7. Another view of Felsenthal's office showing the revealed eaves, which help to dramatize spaces, and the encased columns creating architectural elements.

The biggest problem facing the designers was the lack of light and the claustrophobia inherent in windowless interiors. Skylights were the logical solution, but the prohibitive cost limited their number to three, which were carefully placed to admit lots of daylight. The glass doors allow this light to flow from one area to another. As a result, the absence of windows is hardly perceived.

One of the highlights of the space is the art by Betty Ann Felderman. Her paintings heighten the awareness of the bold spatial elements, while reminding the viewer of the constantly changing quality of light on objects. It is a case of art and architecture reinforcing each other in this imaginative renovation.

4

5

6

7

A three-story Victorian seminary and a Massachusetts architectural landmark dating from 1864 gets a sympathetic renovation that makes it more viable than ever.

Colby Hall crowns a bucolic setting on one of the highest hills in Newton, Massachusetts. Built between 1864 and 1866 for Andover Newton Theological School, it is a local landmark of considerable architectural quality. Today the Hall is more authentic and more viable than ever. Stonework has been repaired, the ground relandscaped. Most dramatic is the transformation of the interiors, now headquarters of the designers who are responsible for the renovation, Drummey Rosane Anderson.

Once gloomy, Colby Hall is now an exhilarating environment. Walls have been removed and stair landings modified into bridges, opening vertical and diagonal vistas through all three levels to the original skylight. Paradoxically, though many of the original partitions have been taken away, significant features of the interior, such as the grand staircase and great hall, are more poignantly evident than before. For example, the carved newel posts and stairway balustrade, original molding and trim remain intact and restored to their former Victorian glory.

To allow the architectural firm to function smoothly, on the second floor over the great hall a design studio of similar dimensions was created from two small rooms. Floods of daylight are free to flow in many directions. For David Anderson, principal and partner in charge of the renovation, the headquartering of the firm here underscores his commitment to adaptive reuse and the firm's approach to such projects for clients.

The building is a series of surprising and satisfying transitions between soaring and cozy spaces. The curving geometric motif of the original architecture has been respected while brought up to date for efficient office use. More than merely coexisting, old and new interact in a counterpoint of color and form.

From his third-floor office directly under the belfry (still in use for the adjacent chapel) Anderson exercises a unique right. He can reach out from his executive chair to the rope that rings the bells. When he does, the peal means that the firm has landed a new commission.

1

2

1. Section drawing of historic Colby Hall, once a theological seminary and now an impressive designer's office. The belfry belongs to an adjacent chapel still in active use.
2. Reception area is furnished with comfortable upholstered seating. A wall of photographs shows the firm's recent architectural design work.
3. Original trusses bisect the second floor drafting studio. A magnificent working space, the ceiling soars to 16 feet.

4. The Great Hall is now a presentation room, with track lighting for illumination.
5. In the belfry tower, principal David Anderson has his office (delineated by the rounded windows).
6. The old grand staircase at Colby Hall is now juxtaposed beside a white curved reception desk.
7. Marketing office has a bright painted niche, effectively fitted with a contemporary workstation and filing cabinets.

5

6

7

Flexibility

Sometimes one space must work for a variety of functions. Flexibility makes business sense today when every square foot is at a premium. Here are five imaginative approaches.

Pentagram

Mary McFadden

James Hester Bates Riek, Inc.

Perry Ellis

Jack Lowery

Pentagram

A seventeenth-floor loft space is stripped down to bare walls to provide optimum flexibility for a graphic design firm that believes in wide-open activity.

Colin Forbes, one of Pentagram's New York partners, deliberately looked for space in a poor state of repair, without landlord improvement, so that it could be adapted to the firm's way of working. The 8000 square feet found in a Madison Square high-rise loft building looked at first like a gloomy crypt that had somehow evolved 17 floors up. Sheetrock partition walls divided the space. Light was completely blocked out by paint-layered windows, and copper framing was similarly obscured. Perfect for a design group that thrives on wide-open spaces.

Architect Katrin Adam swept all partitions away and cleaned up the surrounding shell. Windows were scraped and polished to reveal a view of the sculptural 1910 Groisic building across the street. Copper frames were stripped to their original glowing condition. High up in the grid of ceiling beams, yellow-painted air-conditioning ducts and red sprinklers form a geometric pattern against the pure white envelope. No-nonsense track lighting and gym lockers for personal storage emphasize the high-tech industrial vocabulary.

For such a trail-blazing firm as Pentagram, the nonhierarchical working environment came absolutely naturally. The London office set the pace some years ago, with open-plan furniture systems that adapt for team projects. Since the groupings of people change from job to job, a high degree of flexibility is required in the office. Pentagram designers responded by creating modular table tops in a 2-by-1 proportion. These are set parallel or at right angles and used with swivel or stacking chairs.

Forbes explains: "If there are just two of us working in all this space, we do tend to listen to what the other person is doing. As more people start working, the noise level rises too. So much is going on, we are not disturbed. Rather like newspaper offices where traditionally stories are written in the midst of chaos."

There is just one private area in the communal space (aside from bathrooms). This is the small conference room that doubles as a slide-show presentation area. Even here, though, the Pentagram open policy stresses audible rather than visual privacy, with one glass wall contributing an open look. Large group meetings, are held in the adjacent space, where long tables and stacking chairs provide enough room for 30 people.

Typically, this space is put to work in more ways than one. Every day at 11:30 A.M. chef Robert McElman arrives to start work in the kitchen preparing a buffet lunch. At 1:00 P.M. dishes are set out, work stops, and the meal begins. Partners and employees enjoy democratic-style dining, often with clients.

For Pentagram, democratic flexibility certainly pays off. Clients are attracted, Forbes reports, to the style of working and eating in the open. "We like to convey a message that we are seriously in business and yet not extravagant in our work habits."

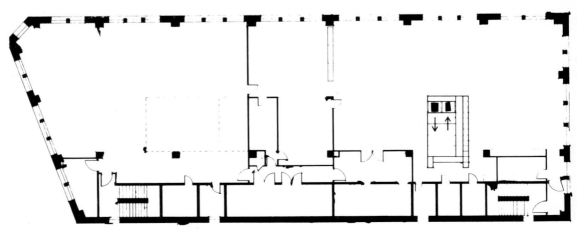

1.   Plan shows existing open office and room for future expansion into adjacent area.
2.   Circular glass portholes present a view into the office from the elevator lobby. Le Corbusier-designed sofas furnish the reception area.
3.   New York partners Peter Harrison, left, and Colin Forbes. Picture shows flexible storage space, far left, which moves on floor tracks and holds archives, supplies and other necessary materials.

4

5

4. Full vista of open workspace. Yellow ducts carry air conditioning. Gym lockers are for personal storage, one for each employee.

5. Efficient galley kitchen where chef Robert McElman prepares lunch every day. He has not been known to repeat a menu for 28 days.

6. Large conference area, which doubles as dining room. Food is set out buffet style on the counter along the far wall. Above are firm-designed pub signs.

7. Small private conference room is the only enclosed space in the office. Blinds pull down over the glass wall when slide-show presentations are made.

6

7

One grand space works as selling area, entertainment room, and principal's office on a level of intimacy that speaks of an individual taste for art.

For Coty Award–winner and American fashion leader Mary McFadden, art and clothing are inseparable. Her body-beautification designs are themselves wearable works of art inspired by the art of many different periods.

The influence of art also permeates the physical surroundings of Mary McFadden, Inc., which are housed on two floors of a loft building in New York's garment district. One floor houses the "behind-the-scenes" aspects of the business, such as the studio and factory where clothing is designed and made, the business offices and McFadden's "nitty-gritty" workspace and extensive art and design library.

On the other floor, however, is the public face of this multi-million-dollar-a-year operation. This is a Fantasyland filled with art and antiques where the designer presents her exterior image, seeing clients, showing new collections, being interviewed by the press, and entertaining people whenever necessary. Lunch is served here to friends and business associates, underlining the trend toward executive offices that are designed for pleasure as well as commercial activity.

The orchestration of color is one of the most impressive aspects of this loft space. The walls and ceiling are painted midnight blue, which contributes a feeling of intimacy to a room of expansive dimensions. Against this background, shapes, colors and textures are arranged with a keen eye for balance and detail.

McFadden travels thousands of miles each year seeking inspiration for her designs from other countries and cultures, and this is instantly visible in her office-showroom. Oriental ceramics, primitive art and hand-woven baskets filled with fresh flowers are all around. A set of eighteenth-century English bamboo chairs flank what must be the most spectacular executive desk in New York—a massive wooden table designed by noted sculptor Mark Di-Suvero which adapts for dining at the appropriate moment.

Art covers the floor in the form of an exquisitely colored Tibetan antique dhurrie, and hangs from the ceiling in the shape of gossamer-wing-like fabric sculptures by Dennis Valenski. Examples of McFadden's own art collection are framed on the walls. It is an ambiance that reflects an extraordinarily creative mind. Because McFadden takes nothing in the visual world for granted, the result is a work environment that is undiluted pleasure.

1

1. In the art-filled headquarters of Mary McFadden, Inc. the gossamer-wing-like sculpture hanging from the ceiling was once in a stage set. The floor is covered with an original antique Tibetan dhurrie. The space functions for multiple activities—entertaining clients, showing fashion collections, and as the principal's working office.

James Hester Bates Riek, Inc.

1. Plan indicates multi-level distribution of space, with design workstations on the diagonal in the high-bay upper level.
2. Exterior of the new JHBR offices, with berming to second level. Impressive glass entrance soars to double-story height.
3. High-pile, brightly colored carpet covers workstation partitions, composed of standard-size wooden doors. Configurations are easily rearranged as project demands dictate. Carpeting provides acoustical control, adds visual warmth and requires low maintenance.

Carpeted doors create an open-plan workstation system that can be instantly rearranged as work teams form and reform.

The offices of Jones Hester Bates Reik, Inc., an architectural firm in Oklahoma City, are the product of an evolutionary process, according to a JHBR principal. The firm had moved its offices three times in the last thirteen years, with each move providing an opportunity to implement new planning considerations to enhance working conditions. Concepts were discarded as they no longer suited the firm's personality and work methods.

For its newest location, as an experiment in design and construction, the firm chose a site in a light industrial area and an interior design program that integrates low costs, ease of maintenance and considerable flexibility.

A multi-level plan separates different functional areas of the office. In the high-bay portion accommodating the design work teams, an unusual system of partitions was constructed. The vertical panels are simply wooden doors of varying lengths and widths, covered in high-pile carpeting. The beauty of this system is that it allows for quick and easy rearranging to meet changing project team requirements. In addition, the use of carpeting adds major benefits in accoustical control, as well as a sense of warmth and informality—characteristics that JHBR likes to emphasize in its daily business.

The inherent flexibility is important to productivity, say the principals emphatically. The resulting sense of openness prevents "staleness and stagnation" among the staff. The playful quality also contributes to creativity. When such psychological motivations are combined with practical energy considerations (interior task lighting, exterior berming), JHBR believes that the work produced by the office reflects an overall design commitment to clients.

1

2

Former banking hall becomes an elegant, versatile headquarters for a clothing designer who needed intimate selling spaces as well as a fashion theater.

In the field of fashion showroom design, there are as many philosophies at work as there are varieties of Heinz pickles. All of them are tied to merchandising strategies—after all, these are spaces for selling, even if on a wholesale level—and all promote the use of innovative design to move the goods. For the Perry Ellis showroom, however, architect James Terrell, of Hambrecht Terrell International, chose the path of least gimmickry, and the results are extremely elegant yet practical, with a modern, flexible selling space and a unique modular, knock-down system for staging all-important fashion shows.

   The architect and client chose the space—a former bank that dates from about 1927—for its grand proportions and impressive windows. It was the mullioned windows, in fact, that had intrigued Perry Ellis for years as he walked through New York's garment district. The space, which had been vacant for several years, had also been "insensitively treated," according to Terrell. Only the marble-faced columns and brass chandeliers were left intact enough to be salvaged.

   Ellis wanted a sense of graciousness to pervade the surroundings; he sought an oasis of calm in the hurly-burly of the fashion world. Added to the question of image were programmatic considerations. The space had to respond to a variety of activities, from quiet, low-keyed selling aimed at small groups of buyers, to exciting, action-packed, disco-beat fashion

1

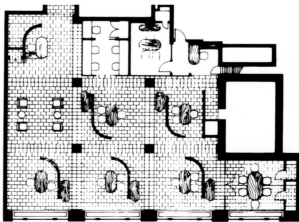

2

1.   Showroom transformed for fashion show via modular runway and seating systems. Additional lighting provides unlimited effects to create visual excitement. Sound system is also suspended from ceiling.
2.   Plan shows selling bays with curved six-foot screens creating intimate areas for small groups of buyers. Peripheral offices provide workspace for sales staff and conferencing.
3.   Typical selling area enclosed by curved screen, with wooden dowel detailing for hanging up garments. Oval table is paired with leather and chrome seating.

4 (overleaf).   View from entrance, with reception desk on right and waiting area for visitors. Existing brass chandeliers were rehung to conform with the original ceiling grid.
5 (overleaf).   Peripheral offices are carpeted and their glass walls detailed with sycamore and chrome.

6. Mirrored wall on right greatly enhances and extends the visual size of the space. On a practical level it reflects models parading on the runway so buyers can see clothes coming and going.

7. Beige marble floor provides an element of quiet neutrality and luxury, considered essential in the marketing and selling of high-priced, couture-level fashion.

shows for crowds of several hundred. Ellis required a runway and lighting and sound systems that vanished once the theatrical presentation was over, so that the showroom could return to business as usual with minimal interruption.

Terrell's solution to this complex request was to create a simple, spare, neutral space, but one that emanates warmth and image from the use of rich materials and spacious proportions. An entire wall is mirrored, thus greatly increasing its visual size. Ondagata marble in pale beige covers the floor area, in a friendly match with the existing columns. Custom-designed selling modules consisting of a rolling unit to hold clothing and a movable curved screen are clad in rich English sycamore veneer. These units, which are six feet high, offer a feeling of enclosure but are low enough to maintain visual continuity within the space. The chandeliers were refurbished, rehung and adapted with up lights, adjustable spots and general down lights to provide all daily illumination requirements. The backdrop of natural textures and colors admirably serves to enhance the clothing, whose rich palette of colors changes from season to season.

Around the periphery of the showroom are the offices of the sales staff. They are extremely small and tightly organized, with built-in desks and cabinetry and a table for conferencing. They are enclosed by a wall of gray glass that is broken by bands of sycamore.

The arrangement for the fashion shows that are held twice a year is designed for rapid assembling and dismantling. Perry Ellis had previously rented runways and bleachers, but rental costs became prohibitive and he wasn't pleased with the visual effect. What he wanted was a theatrical quality but with a cleaner look.

Terrell came up with a system of carpeted runway and bleacher modules that puts the audience at eye level with the models. The modules can be assembled in a day and a half and taken down in half a day. There is space at one end of the runway for video camera, and the mirrored wall at the other end allows the audience to see the models coming and going and also adds to the exciting visual whirl of the shows. Lighting is rented from a theatrical supplier and suspended from a series of anchors in the ceiling. A total of 16 circuited plugs allows for lighting flexibility and unlimited effects.

Behind-the-scenes spaces (not shown in plan) include a workroom where the samples are made, a color room for looking at fabrics under every conceivable light condition, a secretarial area and room for the design assistants.

The philosophies of architect and client in this particular project go hand in hand. They both like to keep things clear and simple—"underdone" is a word Terrell uses. Warmth and a sense of proportion are key elements in their design vocabularies. Terrell likes to be inspired by a space, to take whatever already exists and work with it, developing the solution that meets the client's needs. Clearly, this ideal synergetic situation can produce interior design of remarkable aesthetic and commercial success.

6

7

A multi-purpose, two-level space confined to 18 by 24 feet offers flexibility for work, conferencing, client meetings and dining.

Because of an increasing trend toward in-house dining and the decreasing availability of space, the compact, multi-purpose office is a current design challenge. Jack Lowery, former ASID national president, took up this opportunity recently in a special prototype project geared to a creative woman executive.

Working with a typical space of 18 by 24 feet, with one window wall, Lowery bisected the area with a raised platform placed on the diagonal. He thus created a sense of division and an illusion of spaciousness in a room that is equipped for daily desk work and conferences, as well as dining. The office has its own mini-kitchen, which Lowery predicts may well be integral to many executive office design schemes in the future, just as the executive bath is today.

Dining and conferencing are conducted on the raised platform, around a glass-topped table. The meals are served right out of the adjacent mini-kitchen, which is closed off with a pocket door when not in use. Tucked neatly up against the platform, sectional seating forms the informal conference area organized around a glass-topped coffee table on the lower level. For paper work, the executive operates from a sleek, granite-topped table desk, with an elegant buttoned swivel chair.

When there is no architectural character inherent in an interior space, definitions must be created with color and texture. Jack Lowery went all out to establish femininity in

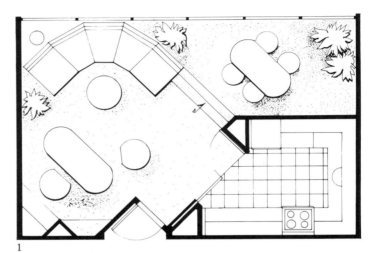

1

2

1. Plan of flexible office, which has four areas of activity: daily desk work, informal conferencing, dining-conferencing and kitchen.
2. Table top set for executive dining. Armchairs are upholstered in velvet for a soft touch.
3. Closeup of the food operations center, a fully equipped mini-kitchen that is capable of producing meals, saving the executive time and money when entertaining with help from an outside caterer.

3

4.   Overview of workspace showing raised platform for dining and conferencing. Kitchen has a pocket door to close it off from the business area.

this flexible workspace, using a palette of rosy pinks and a counterpoint of slate gray. He recognizes that the female business executive is "different" and not the same as her male counterpart when it comes to dress and interior design preferences.

Textures range from the rich, smooth velvet used to upholster the guest chairs, to tactile tweed for seating modules and high-luster steel seen in cylindrical table bases and kitchen detailing. Each element is carefully woven into the overall picture: a neat geometric in rose and white for the carpet, ceramic tiling for the kitchen, even the elegant tableware and crystal for the executive dining table top.

Daylight from the window wall is controlled via thin horizontal blinds, which themselves create a wall of color when pulled all the way down. Finally come the accessories—hand-crafted pillows, an impressive painting and greenery. Lowery adds that he is a great believer in making everyone who comes into a space feel attractive. Warm tones are often the answer for this psychological approach.

4

Prototype

The designer's ideal workspace may never be achieved in real life because of client space or budget restrictions. These six exceptional offices demonstrate what can happen in a totally free situation and give fresh insight into what executive offices can look like.

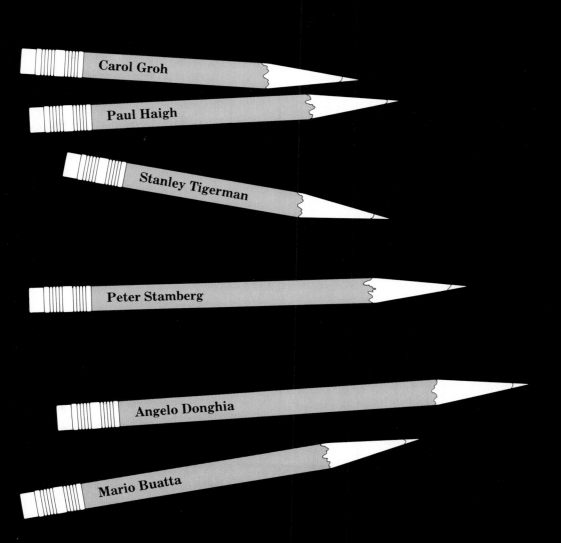

Carol Groh

Paul Haigh

Stanley Tigerman

Peter Stamberg

Angelo Donghia

Mario Buatta

1. Plan indicates perimeter floor tiling and two access doors separated by built-in wall storage that can be used on the executive and adjacent secretarial side.
2. In contrast to the modern geometry of the executive table desk, Chinese-style chairs by Hans Wegner provide a light touch, with seat cushions in silk fabric.

A two-part workplace with the option of conducting formal business at the desk or more relaxed conferencing expresses personal interests and quality through detail and finish.

In 1981, women comprised 27.4 percent of all managers and administrators in the work force. Recognizing the increasingly important role that women play in American corporate organizations, Carol Groh, an architect who is a successful principal in her own design firm, developed this prototype office to reflect the needs of the woman executive. Projecting from her own working methodology, she created a space with a truly executive connotation, very clean, neat and organized.

Groh herself works with a table and a side cube that supports telephone, date books, pencils, and has two drawers for current files. Behind her chair is a desk-height shelf that can be used for display or for work. These elements became central to the design concept of the woman executive's office.

The spacious 20-by-25-foot office is seen as a working-conference room, with a secretarial station in the adjacent area outside. There are two points of entry. The one farther from the desk, intended for visitors, gives the seated occupant a clear view of the person coming in; the second one is intended for quick access to or by her assistant. Between the two doors is a unit of built-in storage, accessible from both sides. On the secretarial side, it contains filing drawers; on the executive side it is used to display objects that reflect the executive's personality and individual interests.

Assuming that the office space is unexceptional architecturally, Groh's design relies on texture and detail to convey a sense of quality and executive atmosphere. Terra-cotta tiles border the perimeter floor and are set off by an inlaid carpet of toning color that defines the working and conference area. Walls are wrapped in custom-designed "stretch" panels upholstered in a terra-cotta fabric to contribute an element of softness. A peach-colored laminate is used to surface the table desk and cube furniture, and upholstery fabric for the conference seating area is coordinated in peach and pale beige.

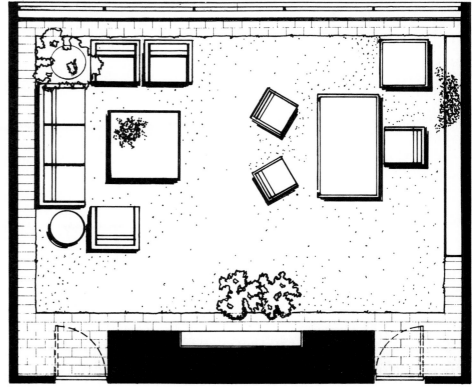

3. Architect Carol Groh in her prototype office, which reflects her own working methods, "neat, clean and organized."
4 and 5. Two views of the conference sitting area, with club chairs and sofa around a cube coffee table.
6. View toward the storage wall unit, which is filled with personal objects that define the occupant's interests—in this prototype, American crafts.

3

4

5

A new slant on the executive workspace places the top manager in an interior office without windows, in an environment that elicits productivity from support staff and conveys subtle signals of authority through the use of classic materials.

The signals in the workplace are changing. The old identifiable status symbols no longer apply as rigidly as before. Summarizing this transition from high-profile personality to participatory manager, architect Paul Haigh produced a management workspace that is revolutionary on many counts. For one, it is a windowless interior space that disposes of the notion that power is measured by square feet of fenestration. What's more, the prototype is interpreted as a total stand-alone object, a shell of sheetrock that can be slipped into any "skin," from curtain-wall cube to industrial loft.

The executive is placed quite literally in the center of the action, with circulation area and support staff on the perimeter of this plan. No doors disturb the progressive environment. Privacy is achieved with vertical blinds that perform as both walls and doors, open or shut as needed. While some may question the degree of privacy, the semi-transparency matches the new barriers-down management theories for effective work environments.

Italian ceramic floor tiles in gray and beige define the executive space, another status twist, but a classical architectural statement, according to Haigh, and one that, through association with grand palaces, cathedrals and other monumental structures, conveys wisdom and history and therefore a sense of power. The

1

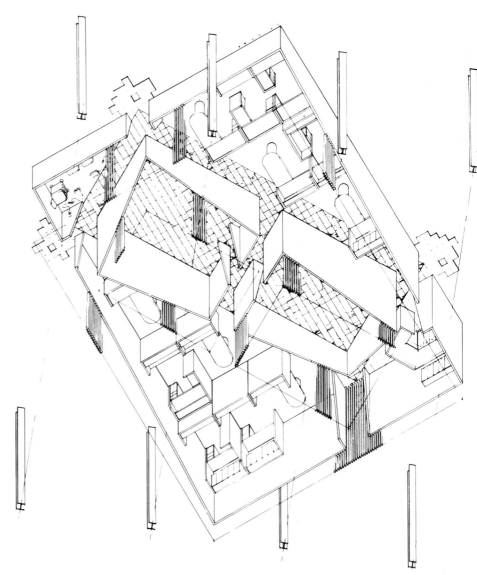

1.   Axonometric shows the executive office and linking conference room placed on the diagonal in a 2500-square-foot area, with support staff at the perimeter.
2.   The stand-alone object is designed to fit into any architectural situation from curtain-wall cube to loft.
3.   Looking down into the executive office wrapped with asymmetrical sheetrock walls and vertical blinds.
4.   Perforated vertical blinds extend to the ground from an overhead suspension rail, to function as doors.

2

3

4

5.   Floor plan indicates workstations for 18 people; the tile-floored executive area has a conference room capable of accommodating eight people.
6.   Three workstation heights show lowest work surface at 29 inches, secretarial station with vertical divider at 42 inches and middle-management station with storage unit rising to 63 inches. Task lighting is incorporated under all the vertical shelving and amplified by individual units on the desk tops.

choice is practical, too, for a business interior when low maintenance and long-term durability are two important requirements. Noise is reduced to a minimum by an acoustical tile backing.

Fundamental to Paul Haigh's design work is the human factor. What matters is how the user reacts to the space. All projects begin from the inside out. In this instance, middle-management and clerical-support workstations were organized logically first before developing any aesthetical "design." Privacy, adjacencies, comfort, communication, lighting and adequate storage were basic considerations. The three different workstation heights selected for the support staff subsequently dictated the cant of the exterior sheetrock walls. The slanting design succeeds in creating an effective visual modulation to the rigid geometry of open offices.

Budget-consciousness must be the mandate for all designers these days, declares Haigh. Creating the basic envelope in sheetrock minimizes costs. Furthermore, this basic material is appropriate in a retrofit situation, which is essentially industrial in its character. By turning the executive core on the diagonal, maximum use of the 2500-square-foot floor area is obtained. Kitchen and waiting area are shoehorned into the triangular spaces behind the executive office-conference area.

Paul Haigh declares that in its determination to reflect the technological idiom, modern architectural design has evolved in the form of Abstract Expressionism, with myth and symbolism rejected and emotional references declared irrelevant. Such fanatical philosophy has diluted the quality of the built environment.

His concern is with reincorporating qualities of coziness, happiness and fun, "realigning architecture with art and nature."

As he demonstrates in this project, the conventional door can be replaced with vertical blinds whose ripple effect reminds the user of primitive door curtains made from rushes or beads. The symbolic welcome mat can be interpreted at the office entry with tiles spilling out of the hall into the recreption area.

The predictable visitor lobby becomes an unintimidating space with up-scale lights and small-scale seating. All these gestures enrich and enhance the working interior.

Wood furniture, wool textiles and ceramic tiling provide an appropriate aesthetic and emotional juxtaposition for the automated office. Analysts specializing in sociological surveys cite the lockstep of high-tech with

high touch, the need for sensuous tactile surfaces. With every advance in technology comes a counter response—well demonstrated in this sensitive prototype.

Emphasizing the new humanity, the executive chair is no longer a formidable throne, the executive desk has dissolved into a friendlier table. Loveseat and armchairs are grouped around a cylindrical wood coffee table for informal conversations.

The companion conference room located opposite the executive office is a serene environment, its table for eight softened with a bull-nose edge. Subtle fabrics in blue and gray upholster the chairs. Because the asymmetrical walls set up their own visual interest, there is no need for decorative art. A pair of Italian table lamps provide the only ornamental touch.

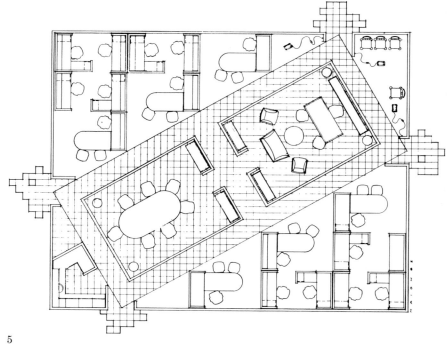

7 and 8.   Sixty-three-inch full height middle-management workstations are upholstered in gray wool fabric. Circulation path is defined in beige and gray ceramic floor tiles, in contrast to the gray wool carpet used in the workstation zones. Cant of the perimeter sheetrock wall is dictated by the various heights of the workstations.

9.   Reception desk with waiting area seen in background.

8

9

5

10.   Serene and uncluttered, the conference room is a place where business can be conducted efficiently. Nothing distracts the eye. Twin lamps on cylindrical pillars are the only ornamental touch.

11.   Executive office is furnished with light oak desk and credenzas. The seating is upholstered in blue and gray worsted-wool textiles. Vertical blinds lead into the companion conference room.

11

12. Kitchen wall cabinets climb the wall to
follow the slope of the asymmetrical sheetrock
envelope. Pantry provides executive and staff
dining support.

13. Reception area becomes less intimidating
with small-scale furniture and up-scale
lighting.

14 through 16. Views from the entrance
ways show the asymmetrical geometry of
sheetrock planes, the floor tiles spilling out as
a welcome mat.

13

14

15

16

1. Yellow brick forms an allée in the office greenscape in which six parterre work bays are treated to a floor covering of ersatz grass.
2. Awnings and street lamps, hedges and clouds, lattice panels help to make the indoors look like outdoors.

A formal garden plan is literally turned inside out to become an executive workspace and a witty pun on the all-too-familiar open office landscape.

The open office has been the subject of study, research, discussion and criticism for the past decade. Since it is predicted that by the year 2000 half of the labor force in the U.S. will be made up of knowledge workers, it seems likely that the open plan is here to stay. Furthermore, as rentals escalate and office organization eases toward increased democ-racy, it seems probable that enlight-ened management will embrace the concept for their own use. For this small prototype alternative to the executive fortress, architect Stanley Tigerman turned to an inside-outside inversion—and thus arose the idea of the office greenscape, a witty pun on the notion of more familiar office landscape.

Tigerman took a list of garden metaphors—brick, gravel, statuary, lattice, awnings, clouds, trees, hedges, lamp posts—all of which were incorporated in the design scheme. The metaphorical pileup was intended to convey layers of meaning for the office occupants and build a sense of continuity between work and leisure.

The space chosen to develop this concept was a storefront loft with high ceilings, sand-blasted brick walls and general "unfinished" look. Within this shell, it was decided that the garden landscape could be for-mal, with an allée and a grid of par-terres. The space is bisected by a circulation path of yellow brick, at either end of which are ficus trees and classical statuary. Six parterres, three on either side of the path, are

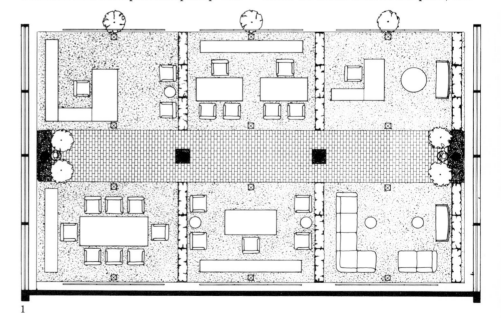

1

3. Reception area seating is comfortable brown leather, augmented with wooden park seats.
4. Italian desk lamps contrast nicely with Philadelphia-style, turn-of-the-century street lamps. Further illumination is added with ceiling track lights.
5. Light oak furniture and white tweed upholstery are in the spirit of the outdoors.

divided by low boxwood hedges into office spaces, with a ground covering of ersatz grass. Overhead are white canvas awnings "sheltering" the furniture. Further defining the individual workspaces are Styrofoam cloud shapes floating over the hedges, to augment the vertical separations.

Turn-of-the-century street lamps add another layer of association to the mix and contrast nicely with the ultra-modern Italian-designed desk lamps on all the work surfaces. The exterior walls of the office are un-painted wood lattice, with cutouts based on classical pediment shapes. This envelope is purposely placed two feet away from the brick loft walls, with a ditch of gravel between, thereby maintaining ambiguity as to whether the brick is interior or exterior. Similarly, because the yellow and white striped awnings are on the *inside* of the storefront glazing, office occupants look *into* the street as if it were a shop window display—an approach that reinforces the illusion of the office as an outside space.

Tigerman's witty juxtapositions are everywhere. A barbecue grill is set beside the reception area seating. Garden hoses, watering can, wheelbarrow and other horticultural implements take their place in this greenscape like Pop Art. Light oak furniture and wool tweed upholstery are in the outdoor spirit as well. While this use of symbols, decoration and layered associations may be readily identifiable as Post-Modern, the humorous character that is a Tigerman hallmark pushes the project to a new edge of understanding what an office may be. Work can be fun: what's wrong with lighthearted surroundings?

3

4

6. Architect Stanley Tigerman and interior designer Margaret McCurry, the "Gothic" environmental designers who created the office greenscape.
7. View from the executive desk toward the conference bay. Statuary and trees help the horticultural metaphor grow.

7

Establishing leading-edge criteria for the executive, this office is designed in a warehouse, with emphasis on energy-saving and a whole new compendium of top management status symbols.

What are the new design standards for the executive office? In the 1980s it is clear that some facets of executive "play" are changing. Gone are the days when the executive retreated into a fortresslike environment, protected by weighty mahogany doors, and buzzed imperiously for attention by remote control. Informality is perhaps the key word in business today. In this office it is expressed through location, organization of space and furnishings.

Architect Peter Stamberg started out on this prototype executive office project by considering location. Because of escalating rentals in high-rise office buildings, adaptive reuse seemed appropriate. He chose a 55-by-55 foot open space in a 1925 downtown Manhattan warehouse, typical of the type that forward-thinking corporations are moving into today. He defined six distinct areas necessary in the executive office—inner sanctum, conference lounge, secretarial area, executive dining room, waiting area and equipment core. To gain maximum use of daylight for day-to-day business, he located an equipment core for photocopying, electrical and plumbing access in the center of the space in an eight-foot cube. The various functions of the office pinwheel from this central point.

Inspired by the functional flexibility of blinds, Stamberg chose to define the separate zones with horizontal chrome/black slats that can be used to achieve opaque, translucent

1

2

3

1. Executive office with dividing blinds open, for visibility through to connecting spaces.
2. Secretarial table desks with credenzas for storage are arranged outside the main executive office, with blinds down.
3. Secretarial area with blinds up, to allow views through to the conference lounge.
4. Designer Peter Stamberg in the executive chair. Overhead fan, rubber floor and flexible lighting denote the rethinking of executive status symbols.

4

or transparent partitions, all with a small adjustment. The blinds are nonwalls serving symbolically to highlight the new executive informality and accessibility.

The particular blinds in this office which are black on one side and chrome on the other are part of a thoughtful energy-conserving design program that further defines a forward-thinking executive with his pulse on sociopolitical issues. Aside from the nighttime contribution of retaining heat, they help to regulate the interior temperature through all seasons. With the black side facing the windows, the blinds absorb heat, increasing temperature in the space. Turned with the chrome facing out, the blinds deflect summer heat.

In Stamberg's energy-saving program, the blinds are combined with overhead fans to circulate hot air in winter, and keep it moving through operable windows in summer. Augmenting the comfort level in this environment is a set of energy rods filled with special crystals to absorb or radiate heat.

Working with architect Paul Aferiat, Stamberg developed a palette of pale gray, with white molding and window frames for the perimeter walls; color is introduced on the new construction within the space— peach, coral, grape, mauve, celadon.

In dividing up the space into six distinct zones, Stamberg amplifies that new predominating executive privilege—in-house dining. Furthermore, the executive dining room reflects the concept of the executive team as an extended family.

Typical of the new design vocabulary introduced by Stamberg, the floor is covered with gray rubber rather than plush carpet. Its grid pattern helps to bring order to the

open-plan office. Lighting pursues the objective of redefining executive symbols, too. A forest of 20 flexible up-or-down lamps is used to create architectural boundaries within each individual zone.

Finally, the formal conference room is banished, in favor of the conference lounge, an appealing space furnished with comfortable sofas around a large, low coffee table. Says Stamberg: "The conference lounge is a place where ideas are hatched." The net result: efficiency and productivity, humanity and energy.

5

6

5.   Executive dining room with blinds open, and a view of the equipment core with its coral-painted wall.
6.   The dining room with blinds down presents a silvery space for private executive discussions over lunch.
7.   Peter Stamberg at the executive dining table, with the blinds open to show their transparency and the forest of up-and-down lamps that illuminate the office.

8.   Conference lounge is furnished with three large-scale sofas upholstered in black wool tweed, arranged around a four-foot-square coffee table. The blinds are pulled down to encourage idea hatching. In the far corner, the energy rods are placed against the wall, to absorb or radiate heat and modulate the interior temperature.

9.   View from the conference lounge into the executive office. The single nod to conventional executive paraphernalia is a Stuart Davis-designed area rug, in front of the executive desk.

9

High tech and soft tech combine in a rich and luxurious office suite to demonstrate the principle of motivating successful business relationships through calculated design.

In any design job, furniture is as important as space and architecture. Yet often it is subordinated to the architectural design. In designer Angelo Donghia's belief, this is a great mistake. The primary consideration should be given to people and their comfort level. When people are comfortable, they relax and feel good. When this level of feeling is reached, they also look more attractive, and thus a state of confidence results that—in a business environment—helps to encourage achievements.

By following this philosophy, Donghia has built up his business over the past 20 years to a point where it now has six divisions involved in design services, textiles, wall coverings, accessories, home and contract furniture and showrooms. As president of such an empire, he must present a public face that is impressive and fitting. The suite shown here was developed as a model presidential office, reflecting his personal ideas of what an executive workplace should look like.

His interior design guideline is the private library at home, a quiet, serene atmosphere with comfortable seating, well-chosen artwork and subtle lighting. In this office, walls are wrapped in dark green plush fabric, and the ceiling, with recessed lighting, is covered with gold-leaf tile. The streamlined executive desk is surfaced in lizard and contains a hidden technology drawer, with telephone and remote control for

1

2

3

1. View from the executive desk toward a relaxed conference seating area, with tub chairs and matching sofa.
2. To streamline the desk top, telephone and other remote controls are built into the right-hand technology drawer.
3. To achieve a hushed atmosphere, walls and reception desk are covered in decibel-controlling acoustical fabrics.
4. Chairs flank the top executive's work area, equipped with a mini-computer. Desk is designed in book-matched mahogany with a lizard surface. Swivel chair is covered in rich leather.
5. Plan of the executive suite shows relationship among foyer, executive office and conference dining room.

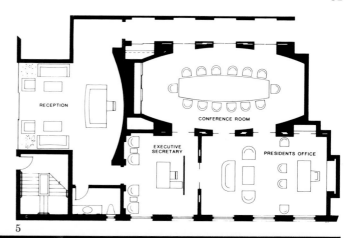

5

4

lighting, heating, cooling and operating windows and doors.

Integral to the Donghia presidential office complex is the conference room. This space is multi-functional, serving as board room, communications center and executive dining facility. To achieve all these objectives required close collaboration between designer and communications experts.

The conference room reaches beyond the function of a room for projecting information from slide or film. It is equipped for city-to-city video-conferencing and for simultaneous showing of film and slides, as well as a live speaker. Equipment records the whole meeting on cassette or disc for future use, which saves executive travel time and expenses. A stand-alone roll-around console unit is used to control the technology. All the electronic equipment is built into one wall, and closed off when the conference room becomes a dining room.

Because people must sit for long hours in the board room, Donghia made a point of introducing curvilinear forms "to soften hard edges." Thus the conference table is boat shaped, and the walls of the room echo the curve of it. Chairs are especially comfortable, so they give the user a sense of floating. A sensor network system addressable on wall-switch panels controls the room temperature as well as the illumination level.

At dining times, an adjustment in the lighting dramatizes the table top, which becomes a stage for fine crystal, silverware and china, reflecting the designer's regard for quality and good taste.

It's really no wonder that chief executive officers such as Pepsi-Co's Donald Kendall call on Angelo Donghia when executive spaces are required. What is subtly created here is a complex that looks decidedly modern and up to date but nevertheless feels traditional (a very important requirement in top corporations whose directors mostly feel more comfortable with conservatism around them).

The Donghia style is also one of familiarity, based on a residential approach: "I see no reason why men and women should not enjoy the comfort and style of their homes when at work." Donghia cautions that we are not in the year 2001— yet. So furniture does not need to look like it belongs in a spacecraft. He likes warm wood and soft textiles, adding that shape is the real story.

His original pieces designed today strive for a classic style that will look as good 20 years from now, will not date or place themselves in history easily. The Donghia touch may be easy to explain but harder to accomplish.

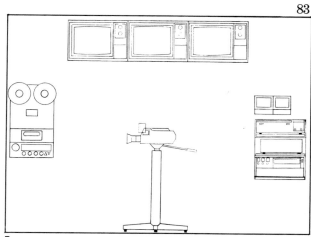

6. The boat-shaped table is designed in three sections, resting on steel cylinders. Pendant lights hang from the ceiling, to augment recessed spotlights. Comfortable swivel armchairs are covered in red plush fabric. The walls of this neutral room are surfaced with a marblized paper placed horizontally to resemble the real material.

7. Conference room/communications center is equipped with a wall of electronic devices, including three video receiver monitors, dual monitoring unit, video disc player, video cassette receiver and player, portable color camera, cassette and reel-to-reel recorders.

7

84 Angelo Donghia

8 and 9. Lunch for 14 set in the board room, which with versatile lighting, acoustic ceiling tiles, handsome textiles and carpeting becomes an elegant executive dining room. Silverware, china and crystal are carefully selected to emphasize the traditional-modern touch. For dining, doors close off the electronic communications center at one end of the room. The door covering matches the rest of the walls in this soft-edged curvilinear space.

8

9

Mario Buatta

1. Designer Mario Buatta in the sitting-conference area of his model work environment. The room is a study in blue and white and pattern on pattern.
2 (overleaf). Overall view of the 18-by-24-foot space, with wood-burning fireplace, book-lined walls and a scattering of personal memorabilia, all of which convey a residential feeling.

A townhouse living-room study project reflects the personal taste of a designer who appreciates the decorative arts but likes to bring a strong feeling of comfort to the executive workplace.

Warmth, quality and natural materials, these are the components that are required in office planning today, according to the latest report from BOSTI (the Buffalo Organization for Social and Technological Innovation). The study notes that 85 percent of people surveyed want wood and fabric in their offices, rather than vinyls and laminates. Pastel shades are preferred to neutrals or bright colors. Overall, the most desirable working environment is one with a homey, comfortable feeling.

In many corporations, the home-away-from-home atmosphere is already percolating down from the top executive level to middle management. The residential design approach offers a degree of informality and comfort through which many people derive inspiration for their work. This office prototype represents this contradential direction.

While it is not the actual workplace of the designer Mario Buatta, it summarizes the elements that he likes to be surrounded with when he is working. It is a style he calls updated traditional. As a noted collector of blue and white porcelain, Buatta frequently favors a palette with this theme in mind, and this workplace is no exception. The space is put together with an intriguing selection of blue and white patterns. There are three different fabrics, a businesslike plaid, a vibrant tree-of-life print and a watercolor stripe. These are played against a blue and white floor (a solid white carpet overlaid with a blue and white patterned rug). The shell that envelopes everything consists of deep blue walls crisped with white moldings.

Comfort and quality are two vital ingredients that Buatta insists should be evident in rooms no matter for what purpose they are used. Particularly for the designer, he maintains, they are the unique selling points of the interior design business. The room, which takes its dimension from a townhouse, is divided into two comfortable areas furnished with a careful mixture of antiques and modern designs. Buatta has learned the value of historical continuity in interior spaces and is a master at capturing the past and wrapping it up in a setting that is essentially modern. The result is a room of extraordinary richness and depth.

The streamlined geometry of a contemporary rosewood desk with matching credenza, plus an L-shaped sectional seating unit placed around a bold, glass-topped coffee table, and the addition of some contemporary paintings are just enough to tip this office into the context of "modern." Other objects convey the spirit of previous centuries of elegance: a pair of Georgian chairs, for example, pulled up at the desk for visitors, the unmatched antique tables against the modular seating unit, an unexpected telephone table and the buttoned swivel chair. On a practical level, floor canisters provide most of the illumination, with task lighting where it is needed.

Books, family photos and other memorabilia and flowers are typical of the little things that Buatta enjoys looking at and having around while designing. The working fireplace is significant in several ways. As well as being a symbol of history, it plays its own contemporary role in the contradential workplace, as a newly rediscovered benefit in times of energy consciousness.

This is a workplace with all the elegance of a luxurious townhouse study, a space intended to turn work into pleasure.

1

2

Image

The workplace identifies the corporate face of a company, sending visual messages that convey its style of operation, taste and the personality of its executives. These eight offices are examples of how image can be defined in very different ways.

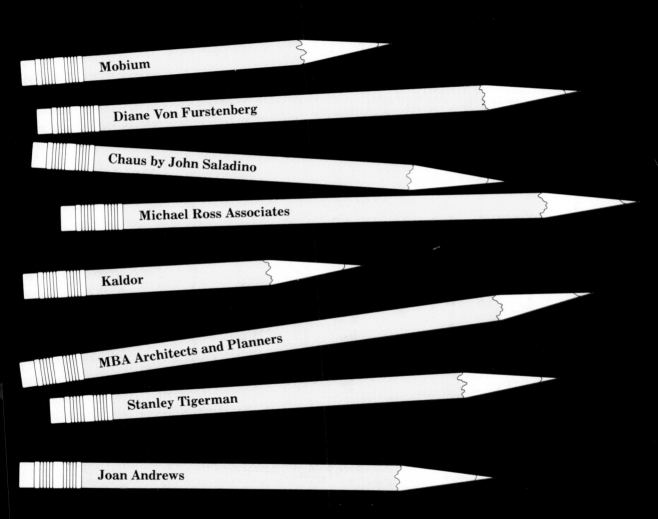

Mobium

Diane Von Furstenberg

Chaus by John Saladino

Michael Ross Associates

Kaldor

MBA Architects and Planners

Stanley Tigerman

Joan Andrews

Mobium

1. Conference room has raised platform and vaulted ceiling. Sliding doors on two sides open it up to the studio.
2. Typical graphic designer's workstation is screened with acoustical panels to create a sense of privacy.
3. Floor plan shows executive offices on the perimeter, surrounding the main presentation area and open studio workspace.
4. An image of quality is conveyed through books in the reception area, which is furnished with carefully selected leather chairs and reading lights.

Strong emphasis on high-quality materials and finishing details pinpoints an office that relies on attracting clients by its meticulous attention to printed quality and the highest standard of graphic design.

In an office that must communicate that the highest standards of quality are central to its operation, Mobium's image literally starts at the front door. This graphic design subsidiary of the R.R. Donnelley printing empire introduces, in its reception area, the books that are printed by the parent firm as leading evidence of good-quality results. Ted Peterson Associates, who designed the offices, placed floor-to-ceiling bookshelves along two sides of the guest sitting space and filled them with an important display of the firm's publications.

In a reversal of conventional office hierarchies, the first thing visitors see beyond the reception area is an open conference room and studio work space. The deliberate juxtaposition of studio and presentation room calls the client's attention to the creative talent behind the proposed graphic design solution.

The conference room where crucial presentations are made is distinguished by a raised platform and vaulted ceiling. Its table, which is built into the platform floor, is a custom design that further serves to monitor the firm's respect for detail and finish.

1

2

For a creative woman in the fashion and cosmetics business, an image of exotic luxury expresses the personal taste of the chief executive and the multi-million dollar company she directs.

The word *sensuous* rarely springs to mind in the design of executive offices, but in a rare instance, as in the headquarters of fashion/cosmetics designer Diane Von Furstenberg, it seems appropriate. The client told the designers, The Switzer Group, that she wanted a mixture of transatlantic ocean liner and Esther Williams movie, and it is precisely that blend of exotic elegance and theatricality that makes these spaces work as a reflection of office image.

The reception area sets the color theme for the offices. Its unusual round desk is banded in signature colors of pink, mauve and pale turquoise. Behind the receptionist, an orchid painting clues the visitor into the company logo. Orchids are also quilted into the fabric covering the banquettes. Satin pillows are tossed informally on this seating. Overhead, the mauve-painted dropped ceiling gives the illusion of reflecting the purple carpet.

Throughout the offices, natural materials were chosen almost exclusively. Most of the carpeting and some of the fabrics were custom-dyed to the client's specifications. Von Furstenberg had strong views about expressing her individual tastes and style. As might be expected, the most personal room is her own office. It is the inner sanctum of a creative, tireless business-woman, and it shows that characteristic vividly. The Art Nouveau desk and a pair of Art Deco armchairs were gifts from family and friends.

The wall behind the desk is a sort of visual laboratory, cluttered with clippings, photographs, sketches and other creative catalysts. White floor-length draperies at the wondows contribute to the "soft office" luxury ambiance.

The cosmetics showroom is the most formal of the office spaces. It is an exercise in Deco sensuality. Rounded corners, pale colors and smooth surfaces combine to form the perfect setting for the display of a very fashionable line of cosmetics and beauty-care items. This feeling is reinforced by the display fixtures and the showroom doors, with their curving handles and portholes (shades of the luxury liner).

The subtle play of colors includes the ubiquitous pale mauve and purple, with an ice cream striped satin fabric used to upholster a banquette.

This is set off with a mirrored wall behind it and mirrored tiles on the ceiling, to give an impression of height and depth. Eight elegant armchairs upholstered in white are grouped around a soft-edged conference table—an inviting arena for discussing the beauty business.

A more relaxed theatrical tone is established in the conference room, where banquettes and chairs are arranged in an area perfectly appropriate to the introduction of new fashion lines and other products. Merchandise is on display on a metal framework and lit with theatrical spotlights for maximum effect. The transatlantic motif is continued in the lights on each side of the windows, which are from an ocean liner.

1. Reception area introduces the visitor to the orchid corporate logo and the signature colors of mauve, pink and pale turquoise. Banquettes are covered in an orchid quilted fabric and decorated with satin pillows.
2. Diane Von Furstenberg in her private inner sanctum. The furniture is Art Deco and Art Nouveau. Soft velvet upholstery and floor-to-ceiling window drapery make this a residential-like workspace.

2

3. View of the windows leading to an outdoor terrace outside Diane Von Furstenberg's private office.
4. The cosmetics showroom is furnished with off-white furniture. The carpet is purple, which creates a dramatic and appropriate effect for the action center of a beauty empire.
5. The conference room is nothing like a conference room. Seating is comfortable and very theatrical, as are the displays of merchandise, which are highlighted with numerous spotlights.
6. Banquette seating in the cosmetics showroom is covered with exotic satin fabric and framed with mirror behind and overhead, to give a sense of depth and height.

3

4

5

Chaus by John Saladino

1. Showroom and offices totaling 2500 square feet indicate principal's office off the showroom space, with adjacent secretary and support staff.
2. Entrance lobby is furnished with antique Irish hunt table. Architectural forms are made of unfinished plaster.

A message of enduring stability is carefully conveyed in this museumlike fashion showroom located in the here-today-gone-tomorrow neighborhood of New York's Seventh Avenue.

In the transient world of fashion design, with its changing looks and fads, the most successful showrooms for conducting business are those that present an underlying feeling of continuity to visiting clients. In this instance, interior designer John Saladino did not go so far as to interpret the surroundings in eighteenth-century French style, although the final result is one of classicism. He used a contemporary vocabulary while drawing on historic reference from Egypt and Italy.

By intent, the Chaus showroom ambiance is calculated to recreate a feeling of a museum, a sheltered and artful place in contrast with the fast-paced world of Manhattan's garment district outside.

Sensitive spatial organization leads from a narrow entrance lobby to a diagonally placed opening to the 3500-square-foot showroom. Quoting Philip Johnson's maxim that spaces should be experienced sequentially, Saladino describes this entrance as the "moment of pause" before the "reward" is offered. The lobby is interpreted as a Venetian canal bringing the visitor to the piazza, the dark and sheltered tube giving way to the light, open, public space.

The cultural environment is reinforced by an antique Irish eight-foot hunt table in the reception area, flanked by a pair of Chinese stone lions. From here the space develops into a voluptuous arena, its classical message carried out in a carefully

coded palette of colors in a range of taupe tones, reflected in polished sheet ceilings that sparkle with exposed spotlights. The neutral envelope here is particularly appropriate in a showroom that becomes a colorful kaleidoscope of clothes, models and buyers during the day.

Making maximum use of existing walls and creating new ones where necessary, Saladino contrived 15 separate seating groups in this space, all with comfortable banquettes or armchairs, sometimes both, for groups of visitors to view the clothes. The armchairs are his own design, inspired by a Roman garden chair made of marble. The upholstery sweeps down to the floor, to avoid a visual forest of legs in a room crowded with chairs. Conspicuous in achieving the desired result of stability and permanence is the use of

natural plaster, which is sculpted into forms and left as the final finish on walls. It conveys a deliberately calculated, subdued atmosphere.

Furthermore, as Saladino has proven in so many previous projects, the introduction of interior architectural three-dimensional forms—architecture within architecture—builds the impression of strength and integrity. All of these qualities not only work aesthetically but serve to reinforce the client's all-important image of having a long-term existence in an industry with so many short-lived names and fickle followers.

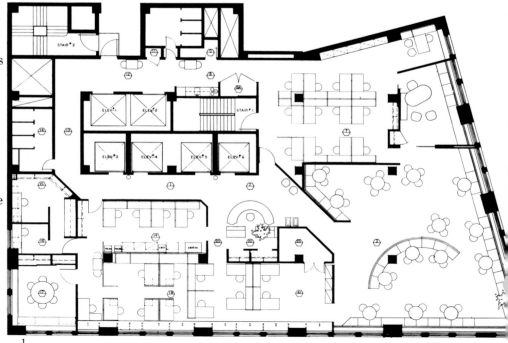

3.   Colorful clothes provide the impact in this neutral showroom, with mirrored ceiling reflecting a host of spotlights.

4.   Josephine Chaus' office, with centered conference table.

5.   Bernard Chaus' office opening off the showroom, with lacquered soft-edged table-desk.

4

5

Michael Ross Associates

1. Axonometric drawing explains the exterior and interior arched façades, which are poised between three arched forms placed on the diagonal.

2 through 5. The cutout archways in painted sheetrock help to form the organizing architecture for designers' workstations. The framework incorporates lighting tubes. Additional task lighting is at each designer's desk and skylights punctuate the ceiling, bringing in natural daylight.

A villa in Vicenza, a local power station and the neon lights of Tokyo are three of the eclectic elements in an office that defines the headquarters of a Post-Modern architectural design firm.

Allusion, ornament and context are the cornerstones of Post-Modernist architecture. Thus it was only natural that a young Post-Modern architect, Michael Ross, should develop all three principles in the remodeling of a classic "shoebox" storefront into his own office.

In this instance, he derived contextual inspiration from the Santa Monica City Hall and power station, historical allusion from Andrea Palladio's Villa Valmarana of 1541 and ornamentalism from the electrographic architecture of Tokyo's Ginza and Shinjuku.

While the sources for form and color are eclectic, the planning approach is more specifically modern in origin. The use of the diagonal, pragmatically more efficient in terms of the number of workstations it can accommodate, activates the space. The office is organized in layers: reception zones, studio and conference-support facilities.

Sheetrock arches span from wall to wall, creating a processional movement toward the end where the conference room is raised on a plat-

form, its arched window set into a curved wall, to form a room within a room. This façade and its exterior twin are painted in strong colors, while the interior arches are in muted hues of violet and pink. On a practical note, skylights punched in the roof emit natural light, which is augmented by fluorescent tubes, themselves an integral element in the sheetrock forms. Architecture within architecture is the message here.

2

3

1

4

Cement-block stairways for fabric displays and an industrial aesthetic position a fabric company as modern and in the vanguard of design thinking.

When Australian fabric importer John Kaldor wanted to expand his Manhattan showroom, he set a tight budget and put a double whammy on "design": only fluorescent lighting and all the samples out for everyone to see, "like a greengrocer's shop." Architect Paul Haigh, undaunted by these restrictions, proceeded to capitalize on minimalism and the industrial aesthetic, which seemed appropriate, since the showroom is in a loft building.

The interior was gutted and all the conduits and pipes in the ceiling exposed. In the center of the space stairways were created of cement blocks, painted white. These effectively provide steps on which bolts of fabric from the Kaldor collection are displayed, replacing conventional "wings" around the walls.

With the goods out in the open and as touchable as fruit and vegetables on a greengrocer's stall, the next objective was to light them for maximum impact. The preferred fluorescent lights selected by fabric designer Kaldor do just that, showing off the translucent fabrics and high-energy prints better than incandescent. Introducing an architectural design element, Haigh organized the light tubes in an alternating sequence of warm white and cool white across the ceiling so they set up their own visual pattern of color and design.

A sheetrock wall that sweeps around the central selling and display space provides private areas for conferences, sales operations and principals. They are quietly furnished with a minimal amount of furniture, the chairs upholstered in black leather. Throughout, the floor is covered with gray industrial carpeting, and the walls painted a silver gray, establishing a crisp monotone against which the fabrics themselves speak out vibrantly.

In the first six months of operation, Kaldor's sales figures rocketed from a projected $400,000 to over $1 million. Paul Haigh won an Interiors Award for his efforts, a Low Budget accolade to honor his achievement in bringing in this showroom at $18 per square foot. Everything happens when you establish the right image.

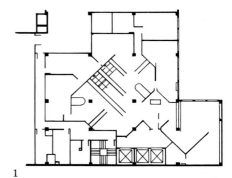

1

2

1.   Floor plan breaks away from the square geometry of the space, introducing diagonal planes to enclose the central selling area.

2.   Conference room minimally furnished with black leather chairs. Bolts of cloth are placed symbolically against the wall. The conventional "wings" are intentionally abandoned.

3 and 4.   The cement-block stairways that display all the fabrics are designed to show off the goods like fruit and vegetables in a greengrocer's shop. Overhead, fluorescent tubes set up their own pattern of color.

5.   Small perimeter office has a window onto the display space.

6.   Reception area with desk in painted cement block like the fabric display stairways continues the industrial aesthetic.

3

5

6

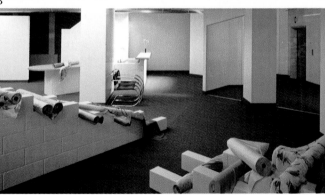

4

A light-filled loft with a measure of informality shows that a design firm's impressive tradition has evolved into a contemporary attitude toward flexibility.

Marcel Breuer is a legendary figure in the history of twentieth-century architecture and interior design. He was made a master at the Bauhaus in his early twenties, and he invented the tubular steel chair. His steel office furniture designs look as modern today as they did in 1930.

Of course, Breuer didn't work alone, and today, since his retirement and death in 1982, his office continues in charge of his long-time partners, Herbert Beckhard, Robert Gatje, Tician Papchristou and Hamilton Smith. The firm's name has been changed to MBA Architects and Planners, and this is not the only aspect of the business that has undergone revision. In terms of style, there is no longer a rigid Breuer "look." While the master's design philosophies are still at work in the office, the individual styles of the partners insure different approaches to architectural projects that they consider very healthy, and have indeed led to an increasing number of commissions for MBA.

All this accelerated activity prompted the firm to change its physical image and move from its midtown Manhattan office space to an entirely new and more spacious location in an older building farther downtown. Capitalizing on the loft architectural plan and breaking away from Breuerism, the designers exposed all the structural and mechanical elements. Gray industrial carpeting covers the floors, and industrial lighting serves as illumination. The organizational arrangement of the

office emphasizes a participatory management system. A central "living room," created with comfortable couches and ample daylighting, doubles as a place to meet clients or for in-house working sessions where objectives and design strategies are discussed.

The message conveyed here is one of tradition tempered with flexibility, important in a situation where there is a danger of being typecast or narrowed down. It's obvious that MBA has successfully broadened its base and used a strategic change in physical environment to develop business growth in step with its competitors.

1

2

1. Reception area with Breuer-designed
Wassily chairs and granite table. Industrial
lights add to the natural daylighting.
2. The conference room with granite table
designed by MBA partners Beckhard and
Gatje and cane and steel Breuer chairs.
Ceiling is painted black in this interior space,
and a structural column decorated with a
graphic of measurements.
3. In the spacious reception area there is
plenty of room to display models of the firm's
work. To the right is the door entering on the
informal "living room."

3

Renaissance motifs, colorful walls and ceiling fans all play an important part in establishing an appropriate image for an unconventional architect.

Architect Stanley Tigerman has never been known to fall in line consistently with any particular design philosophy. Indeed, in his recent book, *Versus, an American Architect's Alternatives*, he explains why he believes there is no clear, one, right way. Just as the human life is made of up of opposites, good and bad, pretty and ugly, so, he declares, are design and architecture. Thus, what seems appropriate at one point may be utterly irrelevant in another.

This has been the case with Tigerman's own workspace. In the 1960s and early '70s, he lived and worked in curtain-wall high-rises in Chicago. He felt an obligation to Mies van der Rohe, the modern architectural City Father who rooted the glass tower in the capital of the Midwest. At this time he had an office humming with people and partners. Toward the end of the '70s, he recognized he had outgrown the desire to be big. Small, he understood, is beautiful. So he changed. He closed down the large office, cut his staff to a half a dozen, and presented an entirely new image.

Not only was he concerned with size, but his attitude toward design and his work environment had shifted as well. He felt it was important to reflect the architectural and social issues of the times. Whatever criticism may be leveled at architectural Post-Modernism, the fact is that pluralism is the name of the game. The old emphatic order of

white walls, no ornamentation and flat roofs is gone.

Today the Tigerman atelier reflects the new vocabulary. It has color, looks back to the Beaux Arts and earlier, but deals with the contemporary concern of energy management.

The space is on the top floor of a grand turn-of-the-century building on Chicago's North Michigan Avenue. It first captured Tigerman's attention with its graceful Palladian-style windows, which open on to wrought-iron balconies. There are eight such windows distributed along two walls. The fenestration itself provided the bones of the design statement for the office.

The sense of historicism was developed by painting all the walls classical yellow. Overhead, an existing domed ceiling was painted with Renaissance blue sky and clouds and them amplified with a touch of twentieth-century Pop Art, in the shape of a suspended super-scale yellow pencil. Workstations are lined up in precise geometry with neat stools, rather like a laboratory bench. Each has an individual flexible arm lamp.

The working configuration demonstrates the new democracy in evidence in forward-thinking offices. There is no difference between Tigerman's workstation and those of his employees. When clients come to discuss a project, he moves to the conference table in the corner for easy communication.

Above all the characteristics of his new workplace, Tigerman is most pleased with the operable windows that allow everyone access to the outside—to be able to feel the lakeshore breezes or step out into the sun. It's a long way from the Modernist school of *climat automatique*,

the hermetic glass box sealed from any outside influence and moderated by complex heating, ventilation and air-conditioning systems. To help disperse the build-up of hot air in the summer, Tigerman installed good old-fashioned ceiling fans.

The final ironic gesture is a transparent column of plastic with a plaster capital containing a floodlight. It sits on the workbench directly beneath the dome, illuminating the celestial painting. This trivialization of such a sacred element as the column not only expresses an attitude toward Post-Modernism, but summarizes the notion of dependent opposites, which are central to his design philosophy.

In Tigerman's opinion, an architect has a responsibility to express the sacred and the profane, the general and the specific, the perpetual and the frail, together but without synthesis. His "one small, hand-held" two-sided mirror view produces original design as exemplified in this particular workplace.

1. Domed ceiling in architect Stanley Tigerman's atelier is painted with a Renaissance vista. The Palladian windows open on to wrought-iron balconies.
2. Super-scale yellow pencil suspended from the dome lends a touch of twentieth-century Pop Art.
3. By the filing cabinets, Tigerman, far right, and team. White coats and bowler hats (seen on the workstations) epitomize the Tigerman approach—witty and serious.

1

2

3

All-out, frankly feminine space for a woman who likes to be surrounded by softness and texture in her creative work.

Can color be integrated into the woman designer's office with successful results? Joan Andrews, a furniture designer, planned her office in a mellow rose to prove it. The color and overall tone of the workspace present a softened image, further emphasized by furniture with rounded edges, comfortable upholstery for chairs and a pillowed chaise lounge.

In a minimum space of 15 by 18 feet, the furniture has been pared down. The desk surface is cantilevered from a wall storage unit made of lacquered wood which has doors covered in hand-painted silk fabric. Chairs pull up to this work area for conferences. Walls are painted a creamy beige, and the carpet is a deep rose that harmonizes with the furniture and fabrics.

This is a functional and efficient space that encourages creativity and provides a warm environment in which to meet clients.

1

2

1. Furniture and interior designer Joan
Andrews at her workplace. The desk is
cantilevered from a lacquered-wood free-
standing wall storage unit.
2. Hand-painted silk fabrics cover the wall
unit's doors, the pillows on armchairs and the
chaise lounge, helping to augment the feeling
of home rather than office.

Living Office

The dual-purpose work and living space makes sound economic sense for the independent designer. These eight living offices range from high-tech to frankly luxurious.

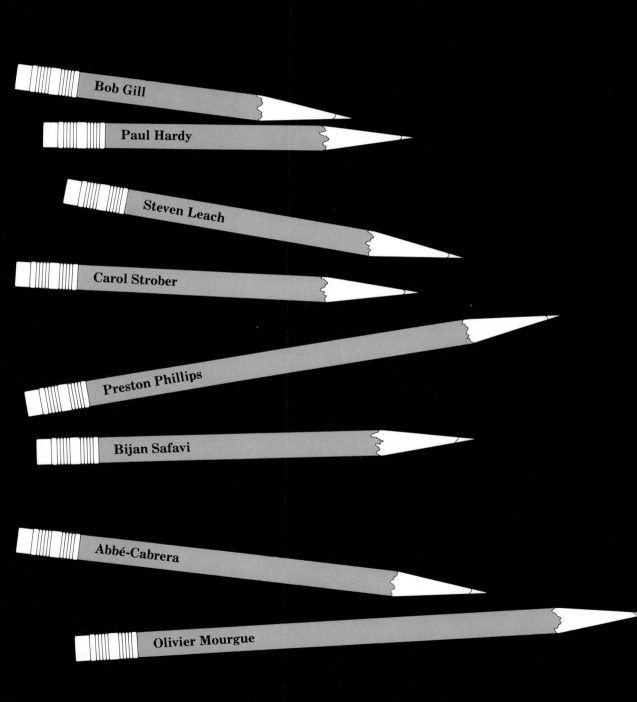

Manipulating a large loft space to create "rooms" that are in reality not rooms but subsets of a single space is a functional solution for a multi-talented person who pursues several creative disciplines.

The Gilsey Hotel was a fashionable Manhattan landmark at the turn of the century, situated in what was then the center of the uptown action, Broadway and Twenty-Sixth Street. When it was bought recently by a firm of real-estate developers that is well known for its sensitive approach to renovation, Bob Gill, graphic designer, theatrical producer and film maker, was one of the first to apply for an apartment in the new loft cooperative. He wanted 1200 square feet that he could live and work in, and he knew exactly how he wanted to develop it.

There are six separate functional areas, yet no full-height walls interrupt the single 12-foot ceiling space, with its generous westerly fenestration. The elevated living area, which contains seating, grand piano and bookshelves, floats on its corner platform, designed with storage space beneath. The "room" for film editing is organized behind a butcher-block bench supported on an old-fashioned map file. The graphic design "studio" is incorporated into the general circulation space that flows between the two areas.

The bedroom is snugly tucked behind a low bed-height wall, sheltered on one side by a high partition that creates a hallway and on the other by the bathroom. To the left of the front door a mini-room that Gill calls his shop provides the necessary spill-over space for bicycles, tools and "stuff." Bathroom and kitchen/dining room fill the interior corner.

The industrial character of the loft is accentuated by dark gray industrial carpet that runs throughout the living office. The exposed pipes, columns and sprinklers pattern the ceilings, and reinforce the character of this workmanlike atelier.

Designing to meet his own multi-personal needs, Gill has nevertheless hit upon a prototypical solution to the problems of a living/working dual-purpose space.

1

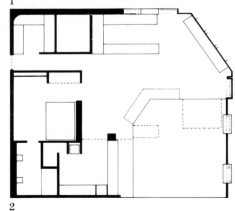

2

3

1. Living room, lifted on its carpeted platform, is lined with industrial shelves. The
giant-size flexible light swings over an Eames
chair. The grand piano is indispensable to a
designer who works on theatrical productions.
2. Floor plan shows the six separate areas
and generous fenestration.
3. Bob Gill is seated in the film-editing
"room." His graphic design studio is located at
right, along the angled wall.

Turn-of-the-century cold-water flat becomes a graphic designer's "airplane cockpit," with a maximum of functions squeezed into minimal dimensions.

Picture a typical New York tenement, cut up into a mass of suffocatingly small spaces, draped with heavy moldings and Victorian encrustations. Then compare such an image with the space pictured here, and you have some sense of the distance separating *before* and *after*.

Graphic designer Paul Hardy had to gut this flat and start from scratch. Walls were removed, the floor leveled, pipes relocated, and layers of paint chipped away to expose the brick beneath the surface. The space was then carefully reorganized to meet the combined living and working requirements of a free-lance operation. (Hardy has a country house to which he travels every week, and so this does not represent his full-time living space.)

Streamlined and efficient, the space is styled with high-tech details and industrial forms. Every element in this designer's "cockpit" conforms to the studio's overall aesthetic. Shelves are supported on invisible recessed brackets. Plumbing and other hardware were discriminatingly chosen to reinforce the image of a person who lives and touches the visual world of today and tomorrow. Lighting is recessed into the new ceiling. Even the radiator is built into the walls.

White, of course, is the watchword here, with graphic punctuations of Matisse red, Van Gogh yellow and Gauguin green, which play off against the natural textures of

butcher block counter, ceramic tile floors and brick walls. Strong poster art augments the scene.

If Hardy's kaleidoscope reflects the taste of an exceptionally creative visual mind, the organizational approach emphasizes the dense-pack configuration of high technology. Every object has its own particular place, designed with the designer in mind. As might be expected in the workspace of a magazine art director, publications receive extra-special storage attention, arranged in a rack with titles all visible at a glance.

Indeed, the overall space of this living office is tuned to the journalistic premise that tight is always better.

1

2

3

1.   Plan of 300-square-foot former cold-water flat shows new plumbing for bath and mini-kitchen.
2.   View from main work-living space down hallway to front door, on left.
3.   Graphic designer and magazine art director Paul Hardy surrounds himself with textures and punctuations of color. Stools and mattress work as guest seats.
4.   Designer's work desk, with adjustable table, light and chair. The butcher block kitchen counter serves as an additional work surface.

4

Steven Leach

For the designer with offices scattered around the world, a home-based communications center is an essential element in the business organization.

Steven Leach is a young designer with a roster of corporate business clients in the Far East and a growing one in North America. He got his first big "break" while working in Hong Kong and from there established branch offices for his own firm in Singapore and Manila. Not long ago he decided to return to the United States and establish his business on home territory. He opened a New York office, which was followed by branches in Dallas and Houston.

With so many connecting points in his business life, he spends a lot of time directing operations via electronic communications systems. Thus, with the necessary mini-computer and telephone modem installed in his apartment, he can work at any hour and communicate around the world at appropriate business hours.

The office shown here is, in fact, a prototype, built for the Annual Designers' Showcase house on Long Island, but it essentially reflects Leach's personal idea of the living office. The space begins with a neutral envelope. Wood floors are bleached to a light coffee color, and fabric stretchwall is chosen to match. Windows are draped with translucent fabric that filters daylight and eliminates harsh glare.

The room is demarcated into sitting-conference area and working-communication zone. For both, the furnishings are heroic and lavish—overscale suede couches placed on a dhurrie rug, a rose-marble oval table desk, leather swivel and bucket

1

chairs, a lacquer credenza. These few but exceptional pieces are complemented with equally exceptional works of art—Far Eastern sculptures and masks and American abstract paintings—all of which are highlighted by spots suspended on ceiling tracks.

Thanks to a highly sophisticated built-in sound system, the ambiance is at once soothing and yet conductive to getting things done. It's a space in which a design executive can catch up with business chores and talk with clients on an informal basis in the precinct of home.

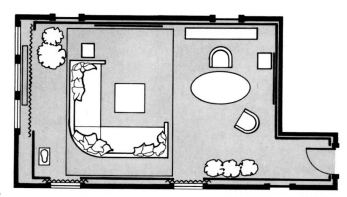

2

3

4

Basement flat in a Greek Revival brownstone functions as the downtown office for a general contracting firm and home for one of its partners.

This apartment is both home and headquarters for its architect/owner, Carol Strober. A central office uptown is augmented by this field post, convenient to downtown New York job sites for the contracting firm in which she is a partner.

The design of this brownstone cellar flat was a challenge. Limited light and space made the plan configuration critical. The concentration of "mechanical" enclosures—kitchen, bath and laundry—against the boiler room walls keeps the living and working space open.

The desk surface is judiciously placed on the diagonal under a window corner. Its storage wall provides a divider for the built-in bed. Seating on the opposite side of the room is also arranged on the diagonal around a wood-burning fireplace.

Details of design play off the massive foundation wall, whose stones were cleaned, repointed and patched. A new ceiling was installed with recessed down lights that focus strategic pools of light over conversation and work areas.

What gives the living office its character, though, is not the expert architectural planning so much as its elaboration and eclectic ornament. The distinctive imprint of an architect and her collections is apparent throughout. An African bedspread, antique dining table, stoneware collection and Irish rug and straw hat miscellany turn the stone-walled basement into a museum of personal artifacts.

1

2

1. Desk surface is enclosed with low storage elements.
2. Kitchen cabinets above a work counter with built-in sink create a divider between cooking and dining areas.
3. From the living zone, the sleeping zone is tucked between the stairway and the work zone, at far right.
4. Plan shows ample built-in closets for owner and guests.

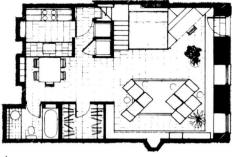

4

3

New York loft is divided logically into an architectural office and an elegant living quarters for a designer who likes to be on top of his work.

Schooled at Auburn, trained under architect Paul Rudolph, Preston Phillips is a young architect who has already built more than 25 private houses for wealthy clients all over the country. What attracts people to Phillips is the inherently modern approach he brings to a project, without any noticeable design derivations from past or present heroic architects.

Like many other young designers today, Phillips decided to be literally on top of his work. So he took a whole floor of a loft building and divided it up logically into workspace for his firm and personal living quarters. What is particularly attractive, however, is that there is no visible dividing line between the two, other than a subtle switch from wood floor to silver-gray carpet. Although Phillips likes to maintain a sense of privacy for his private life, nevertheless there is considerable interaction between the domestic and business areas. Following a meeting in the businesslike conference area, for example, clients often walk into the private dining room for lunch.

A feeling of light and spaciousness prevails throughout this dual-purpose space, along with exceptionally strong artworks. A friend of many artists, Phillips has a collection that includes Lowell Nesbitt, Lynton Wells, Andy Warhol, Buffy Johnson and John MacWhinnie. The entrance foyer is lined with music sheets written by former client Samuel Barber. Modern works belong in such a modern retrofit.

1. Preston Phillips stands between the entrance foyer, where walls are papered with Samuel Barber music sheets, and the design and drafting room, where his team works.
2. Plan of loft floor, with workspace on left and private living quarters on right. Floor levels vary in the private spaces to give architectural dimension and spatial separation.
3. Ficus trees in the conference room, where countertop holds architectural models.
4. Dining zone in the private living quarters. The hallway leads into the working area.

2

3

4

Working out of a typical 1950s modern apartment demands clever space strategy and business-oriented storage for papers and other materials.

Bijan Safavi, an independent architect and furniture designer, felt lucky to find a two-bedroom apartment on the Upper East Side for his family—wife and small daughter—when he arrived in New York from Europe in 1980. Furthermore, it was a rental that was about to become a cooperative apartment. So he seized the opportunity to make what was a boxlike living space function on both a domestic and a commercial basis.

His strategies included turning the dining area into a guest "room" for the child's nurse and carving out a slice of the living room for his drafting and design workspace. Taking advantage of the ceilings in the apartment, he proceeded to add 190 square feet of very necessary extra storage space for work materials, by literally adding an attic built of simple, unpainted, standard-size pine planks, attached to the walls with molleys. The flexibility of this concept allows the shelving to be rearranged easily and also allows quick access to stored items overhead.

Bijan Safavi located the major storage attic above the drafting area. Its lowered wooden "ceiling" served to divide the large open living area from the main sitting area. Green plants seem at home in the attic, spilling over its edges and softening the architectural geometry. With this simple and efficient design, business materials are hidden away but readily available.

1

1. Drafting and design area in the typical
New York City apartment is arranged in part
of the living room.
2. Overhead, pine planks in standard-size
lumber create a storage loft to hold work
materials. Shelves, which are 1″ × 3″ lumber
slats, are entirely flexible or can be removed
for easy access to stored items.
3. Section shows demarcation of work area
between entrance and kitchen and main living
room.

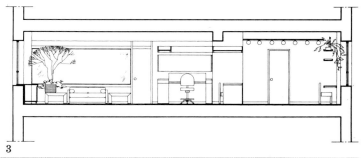

3

2

Modern city apartment becomes a comfortable and appropriate living-working base for two interior designers who like pre–World War II luxury and glamor.

"There is a fine line between luxury and excess," says Dennis Abbé, and he ought to know, because luxury is what his work is all about. As an interior designer, graphic illustrator and renowned glass artist, Abbé has consistently sought an integration of art, design and craftsmanship to create truly luxurious residential and commercial spaces. "People are hungry for richness," he asserts, citing a reaction against ad-hoc and high-tech design. "It's important to make people feel pampered and special."

Abbé has been doing just that for several years from his home base in New York and more recently from a branch office in Toronto illustrated here, directed by his Canadian associate Rafaell Cabrera.

Abbé's particular style anticipated the contradential wave in design and its insistence on comfortable, eclectic interiors not just for residential projects but also commercial ones. So it seemed perfectly natural to locate the Toronto base in a friend's apartment, to consult clients and showcase the partners' own talents, along with those of the artists and craftsmen they employ in Toronto. Furthermore, it provides a comfortable setting in which prospective clients can see examples of the finished product. "Even if the clients' taste differs from ours, they get a good idea of the level of quality at which we operate," Abbé points out.

In this dual-purpose design, the library is used for client consultations, while the dining room serves as a conference area, as well as a pleasant setting for business lunches. The space amply illustrates the designers' commitment to custom tailoring. They developed everything from scratch, right down to the hardware used to suspend window draperies.

The feeling of glamor in this space prevails from the front door. The foyer's velvet-upholstered walls are a vibrant shade of tango, a sort of deep persimmon that was extremely popular during the 1920s, and indeed this era is one that Abbé reflects throughout his work. A capital from the old Roxy Theater in New York, now covered in leather, serves as a console under a lacquered Deco mirror. The front door itself is upholstered in trapunto-stitched velvet and bound in silk cord. In the library, velvet-covered furniture and shirred fabric walls are an elegant foil for Abbé's dramatic window treatment.

Here a painted canvas outer frame and a satin inner frame surround a window made of filigreed paper that is sandwiched between two layers of greenish-amber glass. The design was inspired by one that Abbé saw on a visit to Olana, the home of American painter Frederic Edwin Church.

Across the hall, the dining room is furnished with a custom-made leather-covered table and Jacobean period chairs. Guests are surrounded by treasures such as a gilt-bronze chandelier inlaid with semiprecious stones, silver candlesticks and crystal decanters. A heavy curtain partly separates this area from the living room beyond. It is in this main room that Abbé's special talents are evident in a mural over the fireplace and the opulent carved-glass fire screen, set in a wall of mirror overlaid with a

1. Plan of apartment shows maid's room used as drafting room.
2. Foyer walls are covered in persimmon-colored velvet, and an Art Deco capital becomes a console table, with an appropriate mirror above. Wall sconces echo the 1920s era.
3. Library with comfortable seating and framed window that has a stained-glass effect achieved with paper.
4. Mirror overlaid with a trellis of wood molding is used for the fireplace wall in the living room. Abbé painted the mural and designed the carved glass firescreen.

2

3

4

trellis of wood molding.

Richness is further emphasized in velvet upholstery for sofa and chairs, which are decorated with pillows covered in a needlework appliqué fabric that originally belonged to a pair of portieres from a pre–Civil War house in New Orleans. The ornate character and "parlor" atmosphere is developed with an intricate-patterned carpet and fringed lampshades. In all there are 20 sources of indirect light in this room, consistent with Abbé's view that pools of light make people look their best.

French doors trimmed with bamboo and hung with Chinese lace curtains lead from the living room on to a small terrace, where Abbé designed an awning painted on the inside so that its unique landscape becomes the view. It depicts a night sky, complete with clouds, moon and stars, that is an amusing trompe l'oeil version of the actual sky beyond. The bamboo chairs and floor matting chosen for this sitting area exemplify the theatrical style that is the hallmark of this designer's work.

5

5. The terrace awning is painted with a trompe l'oeil landscape with moon and stars. Bamboo furniture and matting on the floor help to create a theatrical element of fantasy.
6. The dining room performs as conference room, with its custom-made leather-topped table and Jacobean-style chairs. Guests are surrounded with glittering treasures, including a unique gilt-bronze chandelier inlaid with semiprecious stones.

6

Olivier Mourgue

1. Painting bench in the bedroom, where Mourgue works on watercolors.
2. A white seamew marks the Mourgue atelier headquarters. Outside is an ad hoc theatrical stage for improvisational light shows and other community entertainments.
3. Kitchen is equipped with hand-crafted wooden storage.
4. Dining table was constructed from wood left over from the floors after structural renovations were finished.
5. Living room seating area. Stairway leads to bedrooms.
6. The double-height studio with Mourgue at work.

Sixteenth-century stone farm building becomes the new headquarters for a trail-blazing French designer who believes in low technology and renewable energy resources.

An industrial designer who captured the public imagination at international fairs in Osaka and Montreal, Olivier Mourgue might well be thought to be working in an environment of stark white walls and high-tech furniture. In reality, nothing could be further from this image. Today Mourgue has joined the increasing number of creative minds who operate from home. In his own words, it's an "impractical" large old farmhouse in Brittany, near the bracing sea breezes of the English Channel.

The building itself is a spacious stone structure dating back to the sixteenth century. Inside its vast barnlike proportions, he has organized two areas, a double-height work studio for his fabric-design developments and other projects, and living quarters for himself, wife Anne and three children. Skylights are punched through the roof to bring in extra light. The living area functions on two levels, with bedrooms upstairs, and dining, kitchen and sitting spaces on the lower floor. In his own room, Mourgue has arranged a painting bench by the window, where he works on watercolors.

The rough-timbered spaces of his new atelier, the hand-made wood furniture, the relaxed informality of every space, speak of an intense dialogue with low technology and renewable energy resources: sun, wind, earth, water. He manages without central heating. "You live, work, think and sleep better without it," he maintains rigorously.

2

3

4

1

5

Guide to Designers and Resources

Project: Abbé-Cabrera offices
Designers: Abbé-Cabrera
Dennis Abbé and Rafaell Cabrera
246 West End Avenue
New York, NY 10021
Phone: (212) 787-3851

Floor coverings: Canada Carpet Care, Toronto
Custom furniture: Emanual Sidler, Dimension
Furniture, Toronto
Vertical blinds: Irwin Cohen, Toronto
Lighting: City Knockerbocker, Toronto
Awning: Painted by Guy Crittenden, through Soper's
Awning, Toronto
Mirrors: Queen City Glass, Toronto
Wall plaques: Ian Mackintosh, Toronto
Antiques: Renee Antiques, Re-Runs, Edith Nostalgia,
Prince of Serendip, Toronto

Photography by Terry & Ian Samson

Project: Joan Andrews office
Designer: Joan Andrews, Charles Craig Furniture
979 Third Avenue
New York, NY 10022
Phone: (212) 758-3430

Furniture: Charles Craig, New York, NY
Carpet: Kenmore, New York, NY

Photography by Roger Bester

Project: Prototype office by Maria Buatta
Designer: Mario Buatta
120 East 80th Street
New York, NY 10021
Phone: (212) 988-6811

Furniture: Dunbar, Berne, Indiana
Fabrics: Brunschwig & Fils, Clarence House,
New York, NY
Window blinds: Levolor Lorentzen, Lyndhurst, NJ
Lighting: Boyd, San Francisco, CA; Paul M. Jones,
Harry Gitlin, New York, NY
Carpet: Mira-X, Stark, New York, NY
Antiques: Stair & Co., New York, NY
Custom étageres: Royal Brass, New York, NY
Paintings: Andrew Crispo, Andre Emmerich,
New York, NY

Photography by Roger Bester

Project: Vito Cetta offices
Designers: Vito Cetta & Associates
1419 Second Street
Santa Monica, CA 90401
Phone: (213) 452-8491
Lighting: G. J. Neville, Los Angeles, CA
Furniture: Custom fabricated by Heavy Tables,
Los Angeles, CA

Photography by Bert Kaltman

134

Project: Chaus showroom
Designer: John Saladino Inc.
305 East 63rd Street
New York, NY 10021
Phone: (212) 752-2440

Project architect: Douglas E. Brandt, AIA
Furniture: Furniture Consultants Inc., Knoll, Howe, ASI/Intrex, New York, NY; Harter, Sturgis, MI; Storwal, Chicago, IL; David-Edward, Baltimore, PA
Carpet: Stratton, Cartersville, GA
Window blinds: Louver-Drape, Santa Monica, CA
Lighting: Habitat, Harry Gitlin, New York, NY; Lightolier, Jersey City, NJ
Ceiling: Simplex, Hoboken, NJ
Fabrics: Knoll, New York, NY; Kravet, Bethpage, NY

Photography by Peter Paige

Project: Prototype office by Angelo Donghia
Designer: Donghia Associates
315 East 62nd Street
New York, NY 10021
Phone: (212) 759-7777

Furniture: Donghia Furniture, New York, NY
Ceiling: Armstrong Industries, Lancaster, PA
Carpet: Armstrong Industries, Lancaster, PA
Lighting: Lightolier, Jersey City, NJ; Cedric Hartman
Fabrics: Donghia Textiles, New York, NY
Wallcoverings: Armstrong Industries, Lancaster, PA; Donghia Textiles, New York, NY
Table setting: Tiffany, New York, NY
Audiovisual wall: Jim Sant'Andrea Inc., New York, NY
Pocket door covering: Chemetal
Desk drawer control: Audio Command systems
Art: Andrew Crispo, Charles Cowles, Karl Springer, New York, NY
Neocon sculpture: Let There Be Neon, New York, NY

Photography by Michael Dunne

Project: Drummey Rosane Anderson offices
Designers: DRA Architects
141 Herrick Road, P.O. Box 299
Newton Centre, MA 02159
Phone: (617) 964-1700

Carpeting: Milliken, Spartanburg, NC
Lighting: Lightolier, Jersey City, NJ; Columbia, Spokane, WA; Habitat, New York, NY; Staff Lighting, Highland, NY
Tackboards: Armstrong Industries, Lancaster, PA
Furniture: Herman Miller, Zeeland, MI; ICF, New York, NY
Fabrics: Knoll, New York, NY
File cabinets: All-Steel, Aurora, IL; Herman Miller, Zeeland, MI

Photography by Peter Vanderwarker

Project: Perry Ellis Sportswear Inc.
Designer: Hambrecht Terrell
401 East 37th Street
New York, NY 10016
Phone: (212) 683-4550

Principal in charge: James E. Terrell, AIA
Lighting consultant: Jules Fischer & Paul Marantz, New York, NY
Custom fabricator: Anton Waldman Associates, New York, NY
Chairs: Knoll, New York, NY; Herman Miller, Zeeland, MI

Photography by Michael Datoli

Project: ELS Design Group
Designers: ELS Design Group
2040 Addison Street
Berkeley, CA 97404
Phone: (415) 549-2929

Principals: Barry Elbasani, Donn Logan, Michael
Severin
Design team: David Baker, Wendy Tsuji, Marie Fisher
Energy design consultant: Sol-Arc, San Francisco, CA
Carpet: General Felt Industries, Saddle Brook, NJ
Wire shelving: Metropolitan, San Francisco, CA
Drafting stools, desk chairs: Herman Miller,
Zeeland, MI
Window blinds: Levolor, Hoboken, NJ
Lamps: Luxo, Port Chester, NY

Photography by Alan Ohashi

Project: ASE Furno Inc.
Designer: Robert G. Furno, ASE Furno Inc.
17 North Avenue
Norwalk, CT 06851
Phone: (203) 846-4356

Carpeting: Milliken, Spartanburg, NC
Wallcovering: Guilford
Window blinds: Levolor, Hoboken, NJ
Furniture: Artopex, Laval, Quebec, Canada

Photography by Joseph Beignolo

Project: Stanley Felderman offices
Designers: Stanley Felderman Ltd.
711 Fifth Avenue
New York, NY 10022
Phone: (212) 838-0223

Carpeting: Century Carpet
Flooring: Kentile, Brooklyn, NY
Furniture: Knoll, Stendig, Atelier, International,
New York, NY; Delwood, Leeds, AL
Custom fabricators: Arthur Becofsky, Joseph Tekits
Woodworking, New York, NY

Photography by Peter Aaron, ESTO

Project: Bob Gill home office
Designer: Bob Gill
1200 Broadway
New York, NY 10011
Phone: (212) 689-3229

Carpeting: Carpet Loft Inc., New York, NY
Lounge chairs: Herman Miller, Zeeland, MI
Lighting: Lightolier, Jersey City, NJ

Photography by Jon Naar

Project: Prototype office by Carol Groh
Designers: GN Associates
595 Madison Avenue
New York, NY 10022
Phone: (212) 935-2900

Carpeting: Bentley Carpet Mills, City of Industry, CA
Floor tiles: Franciscan Ceramics, Los Angeles, CA
Wallcovering: Stretchwall by Joel Berman,
New York, NY
Fabrics: Boris Kroll, Scalamandre, Brunschwig & Fils,
Knoll International, Jack Lenor Larsen, New York, NY
Laminates: Lamin-Art, Los Angeles, CA

Photography by Roger Bester

Project: Living office by Paul Hardy
Designer: Paul Hardy
325 West 21st Street
New York, NY 10011
Phone: (212) 741-0427

General contractor: Timothy Wildes, New York, NY
Flooring: Franciscan Tile, Los Angeles, CA
Lighting: Lightolier, Jersey City, NJ
Worktable: Bieffe from Sam Flax, New York, NY
Chairs, stools: Beylerian, New York, NY
Storage cart: Intergraph, New York, NY
Files: Charrette, New York, NY

Photography by Jon Naar

Project: Prototype office by Paul Haigh
Designer: Paul Haigh
242 East 62nd Street
New York, NY 10021
Phone: (212) 753-7384

Furniture: Modern Mode, Oakland, CA
Ceramic flooring: Marazzi, USA, Dallas, TX
Partition blinds: LouverDrape, Los Angeles, CA
Carpet: Knoll Floorcarpeting, New York, NY
Reception area seating: Cramer Industries,
Kansas City, KS
Textiles: DesignTex, New York, NY
Lighting: Atelier International, New York, NY
Kitchen: St. Charles Kitchens, New York, NY
Accessories: Smith Metal Arts, Buffalo, NY

Photography by Michael Dunne

Project: Offices of Jones, Hester, Bates, Riek, Inc.
Designer: Jones, Hester, Bates, Riek, Inc.
6525 North Classen
Oklahoma City, OK 73116
Phone: (405) 848-6701

Carpet: Bigelow, Greenville, SC
Pavers: Acme Brick, Brooklyn, NY
Ceilings: U.S. Gypsum, Oconomowoc, WI
Lighting: Columbia, Spokane, WA
Furniture: Vecta, Dallas, TX; Steelcase,
Grand Rapids, MI

Photography by Jones Hester Bates Riek, Inc.

Project: John Kaldor office/showroom
Designer: Paul Haigh
242 East 62nd Street
New York, NY 10021
Phone: (212) 753-7384

Furniture: Knoll International,
New York, NY
Blinds: Levolor, Lyndhurst, NJ
Lighting: Stan Deutsch, New York, NY
Carpet: Ardee Floor Covering

Photography by Bo Parker

Project: Prototype office by Jack Lowery
Designer: Jack Lowery & Associates Inc.
315 East 70th Street
New York, NY 10021
Phone: (212) 734-1680

Furniture: Dunbar, Berne, IN; Intrex, New York, NY
Fabrics: Stroheim & Romann, New York, NY
Carpet: Kenmore, New York, NY
Ceramic tiles: Hastings, Lake Success, NY
Kitchen cabinets: Poggenpohl, Teaneck, NJ
Window blinds: Bali, Montoursville, PA

Photography by Roger Bester

Project: Living office by Steven Leach
Designer: Steven Leach Associates
2 Park Avenue
Suite 2306
New York, NY 10016
Phone: (212) 689-9610

Desk, credenza, sofa: Knoll International, New York,
NY
Coffee table: Scope, New York, NY
Wall and window treatment: Joel Berman,
New York, NY
Fabrics: Kravet, Bethpage, NY; Knoll, New York, NY
Chairs: Zographos, New York, NY
Lighting: Lightolier, Jersey City, NJ
Desk accessories: Smokador, Roselle, NJ

Photography by Roger Bester

Project: Offices of Marion, Cerbatos & Tomasi
Designer: Marquis Associates
243 Vallejo Street
San Francisco, CA 94111
Phone: (415) 788-2644

Floor tiles: American Olean, Lansdale, PA
Window blinds: Levolor, Lyndhurst, NJ
Lighting: Lite Control, San Francisco, CA
Ceiling: Celotex Corp., Tampa, FL
Wallcoverings: Martin-Senour, Cleveland, OH

Photography by Peter Aaron/ESTO

138

Project: Offices of MBA Architects and Planners
Designer: MBA Architects and Planners
15 East 26th Street
New York, NY 10010
Phone: (212) 696-2300

Carpet: J & J Industries, Dalton, GA
Seating: Stendig, Knoll International, ICF,
New York, NY
Window shades: Joel Berman, New York, NY
Granite tables: Cold Spring Granite Co.,
Cold Spring, MN

Photograph by Jon Naar

Project: Offices of Mobium
Designer: Ted Peterson Associates
21 Spinning Wheel Lane
Hindsdale, IL 60521
Phone: (312) 920-1091

Partition system: GF Business Equipment,
Youngstown, OH
Seating: Stendig, New York, NY; Herman Miller,
Zeeland, MI; J. G., Quakertown, PA
Desks, tables, wallstorage: Contemporary American
Furniture, Chicago, IL
Carpet: Strattong Industries, Cartersville, GA

**Photography by Balthazar Korab and Timothy
Hursley**

Project: Office of Mary McFadden
Designer: Mary McFadden
264 West 35th Street
New York, NY 10001
Phone: (212) 736-4078

Photography by Jon Naar

Project: Olivier Mourgue studio
Designer: Olivier Mourgue
Keralio
Par Plougiel
Cotes du Nord
France 2222

Photograph by Patrick Degommier

Project: Pentagram offices
Designer: Katrin Adam
40 West 27th Street
New York, NY 10001
Phone: (212) 685-3027

Furniture: GF Business Equipment, Youngstown, OH;
Krueger, Green Bay, WI; Atelier International,
New York, NY
Carpet: Interface Flooring, LaGrange, GA
Lighting: Lightolier, Jersey City, NJ
Ceramic tiling: American Olean, Lansdale, PA
Hardware: The Ironmonger, Chicago, IL

Photography by Jon Naar

Project: Offices of Ross/Wou Associates
Designer: Michael Ross
826 Pico Boulevard
Santa Monica, CA 90405
Phone: (213) 392-3963

Carpet: Stratton Industries, Cartersville, GA
Tile: Flexco, Tuscumbia, AL
Window blinds: Levolor, Lyndhurst, NJ
Lighting: Halo, Elk Grove, IL; Luxo Lamp Corp.,
Port Chester, NY
Furniture: Krueger, Green Bay, WI
Hardware: Schlage, San Francisco, CA

**Photography by Tim Street Porter, Marvin Rand and
Ave Pildas**

Project: Office of Preston Phillips
Designer: Preston Phillips
17 East 16th Street
10th Floor
New York, NY 10003
Phone: (212) 691-1555

Conference and dining tables: Saporiti/Italia,
New York, NY
Chairs: Stendig, New York, NY
Couches: Keller Williams, Oklahoma City, OK
Track lighting: Halo, Elk Grove, IL
Window blinds: LouverDrape, Los Angeles, CA

Photography by Jon Naar

Project: Living office of Bijan Safavi
Designer: Bijan Safavi
45 East End Avenue
New York, NY 10028
Phone: (212) 734-2844

Lighting: Luxo Lamp Corp., Port Chester, NY
Steel: Cramer Industries, Kansas City, KS

Photography by Jon Naar

Project: Prototype office by Peter Stamberg
Designer: Peter Stamberg
126 Fifth Avenue
New York, NY 10011
Phone: (212) 255-4173

Furniture: Monarch, High Point, NC
Window blinds: Levolor, Lyndhurst, NJ
Flooring: Flexco, Tuscumbia, AL
Lighting: Atelier International, New York, NY
Floor tiling: American Olean, Lansdale, PA
Office accessories: Full Office Furniture,
Long Island City, NY
Rug: V'Soske, New York, NY

Photography by Jon Naar

Project: Prototype office by Stanley Tigerman
Designer: Stanley Tigerman, Michael Abbott,
Margaret McCurry
920 North Michigan Avenue
Chicago, IL 60611
Phone: (312) 642-3665

Furniture: Davis Furniture, High Point, NC
Floorcovering: Astroturf by General Felt Industries,
Saddle Brook, NJ
Brick pavers: Gail Tile, Orange, CA
Lighting: Artemide, New York, NY
Desk accessories: Smokador, Roselle, NJ

Photography by Balthazar Korab

Project: Office of Carol Strober
Designer: Carol Strober
463 West 21st Street
New York, NY 10011
Phone: (212) 874-6593

Furniture: Knoll International, Beylerian,
New York, NY; Sunar, Norwalk, CT
Lighting: Lightolier, Jersey City, NJ; Artemide,
Habitat, New York, NY

Photography by Jon Naar

Project: Stanley Tigerman offices
Designer: Stanley Tigerman
920 North Michigan Avenue
Chicago, IL 60611
Phone: (312) 642-3665

Lighting: Luxo Light Corp., Port Chester, NY

Photography by Barbara Karant

Project: Offices of Diane Von Furstenberg Inc.
Designer: The Switzer Group
515 Madison Avenue
New York, NY 10022
Phone: (212) 759-6280

Edited by Stephen A. Kliment and Susan Davis

Designed by Pentagram

Graphic production by Ellen Greene

Set in 10 point Century Expanded